Managing Creativity

For over a century, creativity has unfolded as a valuable field of knowledge. Emerging from disciplines like psychology, management and education, the field of creativity is making strides in others including the arts and engineering. Research and education in this field helped it establish an identity as evidenced by a growing number of courses and specialised journals. However, this progress has come with a price. In a domain like management, institutionalisation of creativity in learning, research and practice has left creativity subordinated to concerns with standardisation, employability and economic growth. Values like personal fulfilment, uncertainty, improvement and connectedness which could characterise systemic views on creativity need to be rescued to promote more and inclusive dialogue between creativity stakeholders.

The author aims to recover the importance of creativity as a systemic phenomenon and explores how applied systems thinking, or AST, can further support creativity. This demonstrates how creative efforts could be directed to improve quality of life for individuals as well as their environments. The book uses the systems idea as an *enquiring device* to bring together different actors to promote reflection and action about creative possibilities. The chapters offer conceptualisations, applications and reflections of systems ideas to help readers make sense of the field of creativity in academia and elsewhere.

Complemented by the author's own personal, conceptual and practical journey, the insights of the book will act as a vital toolkit for management researchers, career-driven students, practitioners and all creators to define and pursue creative ideas and thrive through their journeys to benefit themselves, other people and organisations.

José-Rodrigo Córdoba-Pachón (systems engineer, MA, PhD, FHEA) is a Senior Lecturer in Technology and Information Management at the School of Management of Royal Holloway University of London, UK, and is also the co-founder of the Technology and Governance Network (TGN), an interdisciplinary group of researchers and practitioners interested in studying links between technology and human emancipation. He has a long-standing interest in applied systems thinking. Prior to becoming an academic in the UK, he was an entrepreneur, software developer and project analyst in Colombia, his native country. He has published extensively in the use of systems thinking to explore complex situations in different realms of life.

Systems Thinking

Series Editors:

Gerald Midgley
University of Hull, U.K.

Systems thinking theory and practice are gaining ground in the worlds of social policy and management. Leaders and decision-makers in an increasingly globalised and developed world are tasked with finding solutions for 'wicked' (highly complex and conflictual) problems, both their organisations and beyond.

The Routledge systems thinking series is designed to make this complex subject as easy for busy practitioners and researchers to understand as possible. It provides a range of reference books, textbooks and research books on a range of themes in systems thinking, from theoretical introductions to the systems thinking approach and its history, through practical guides to the implementation of systems thinking in the world, through to in depth case studies that are significant for their profound impact.

This series is an essential reference point for anyone looking for innovative ways to effect systemic change, or engaging with complex problems.

Managing Creativity
A Systems Thinking Journey
José-Rodrigo Córdoba-Pachón

For more information about this series, please visit: www.routledge.com/Systems-Thinking/book-series/STHINK

Managing Creativity
A Systems Thinking Journey

José-Rodrigo Córdoba-Pachón

LONDON AND NEW YORK

First published 2019
by Routledge

2 Park Square, Milton Park, Abingdon, Oxfordshire OX14 4RN
52 Vanderbilt Avenue, New York, NY 10017

Routledge is an imprint of the Taylor & Francis Group, an informa business

First issued in paperback 2020

British Library Cataloguing-in-Publication Data
A catalogue record for this book is available from the British Library

Library of Congress Cataloging-in-Publication Data
A catalog record has been requested for this book

ISBN: 978-1-138-50021-1 (hbk)
ISBN: 978-0-367-66351-3 (pbk)

Typeset in Bembo
by Apex CoVantage, LLC

To my children Fabrizio and Sofia

*Thank you for choosing me . . . for including me in your games
and in your worlds . . . for showing me the joy in dancing in circles,
discovering snails, throwing water at the sky, crying over a waffle with
no jam or preparing makeshift sleepovers.*

*There are no boundaries, only rules, we can invent them or change
them as we go along.*

Let's pretend, let's create

¿vale?

To my dad

The teacher, the gardener, the lawyer, the manager . . .

Thank you for being yourself, always

Contents

Figures

Tables

Acknowledgements

I would like to thank many people for helping me throughout the journey of writing this book.

To my wife, Cecilia, and my twins, Fabrizio and Sofia, for your unconditional support and understanding. This book is a testament to our daily lives in the past few years.

To the rest of my family (Caya, Xime, Mother and Ricardo). Thanks to Ricardo for sharing his wisdom on creativity at Universidad de los Andes in Bogotá in June 2016. Also thanks to Gerald, Wendy and Luis for encouraging me to develop my ideas on creativity.

To Sue, Jane, Tasha, John, Paul, Christine, Jenny, Pat, Brian, Eddie and many other participants from the activities of CornerHouse Ltd. Your advice and conversations have been always very valuable not only to write this book but to help me improve my well-being.

To the School of Management of Royal Holloway, University of London, for allowing me to create a space to talk about creativity, and for giving me time to write the manuscript. I have become someone else from the person who arrived here ten years ago.

To Kristina Abbotts, Laura Hussey and Christiana Mandizha from Taylor and Francis for their fantastic support during the publishing process.

And last but not least to my students on both sides of the Atlantic Ocean. Thanks to your experiences I am able to better understand creativity, yourselves and myself.

To the reader

This book reflects my research in the last few years, in which, intentionally or not, I have combined experiences of reading and writing about creativity with my teaching encounters with wonderful students and my desire to do something as a systems thinker.

In this combination I have perhaps become less theoretical or academic discipline (information systems, creativity or sustainability) oriented whilst rediscovering my interest in systems thinking and the importance of living it.

Whether the content of this book chimes in with your own reflections and experiences on creativity, I invite you to follow your own journey and not to worry too much if such a journey is a collage of experiences, some of them bigger or more significant than others. I hope by the end of the book you do not see much of a difference between them, between you, me or anyone else.

Enjoy!

JR

Introduction

Several years ago, my wife and I decided to make a change in our lives. This mainly involved moving our jobs, being close to a world metropolis and starting a family. A new academic position in a management (not business) school would help me engage with researchers and practitioners in diverse areas of knowledge. I ventured to go 'out there' and use my systems thinking and information and communications technology (ICT) expertise in new settings.

As time went by I began to think about how different academic disciplines could maintain their status in the face of rapid changes and increasing pressures, one of which is engaging in *inter-disciplinary work*. In most of my efforts to carry out this type of work I would notice an initial degree of creativity followed by some conversations, joint seminars, student supervisions or project bids. Afterwards, myself and collaborators became absorbed by our own demands to manage our research productivity within the academic departments that initially hired us. We needed to show tangible outputs in our own territories. Job and family pressures meant that I had to choose what was most convenient to do. No more time for blue-sky thinking. No time for fighting over egos either.

Worldwide, management education has gone in the direction of prioritising areas like digital innovation or entrepreneurship. Universities in the UK are investing highly in infrastructure and cutting-edge technology facilities with a view to accelerate delivery. Success or failure in quickly getting students into a job often becomes a priority, at the expense of encouraging them to think broadly. Where creative thinking takes place, it is often confused with problem solving in the service of narrowly defined interests.

This means that students and academics interested in creativity, research funding bodies, and public and private sector managers often must fully subordinate their creative ideas to what is trendy, what is commercially attractive or, what is worse for me, what seems to inevitably happen with or without our participation or explicit consent. There are subtle boundaries being wrapped around inter-disciplinary research or education. We identify some of these only when targets are imposed, bids and proposals are rejected or funding allocated.

My own pressures to help put more bums on seats (making a systems thinking course viable to run) have led me to enter the field of creativity. The need to be creative has also led me to notice an increase in the degree of anxiety in myself and students. We have all joined the race to perfection that does not seem to stop and is continuously fuelled by social media.

Whose responsibility is this situation? What can we do about it?

To address these questions, this book explores how applied systems thinking (AST) can further support creativity. Under different names and as subscribed to in more traditional disciplines (psychology, education, management, etc.) creativity is being regarded as a 'new' or 'emerging' scientific field or discipline (Runco and Albert, 2010), one which could help people identify and connect the dots that are in front of us and we cannot or do not want to see. For its part, AST is a body of knowledge that has found its home in management and business education (Jackson, 2003; Midgley, 2000). Its aim is to improve situations with the help of ideas, concepts and methodologies. Central to AST is the systems notion which could be used to conceive of situations as complex and the by-product of relations between elements.

A complementary dialogue between these two bodies of knowledge is proposed and developed in this book through an enrichment of the systems model of creativity initially proposed by Csikszentmihalyi (1988). This model conceives of creativity as residing in several elements (individuals, domains and fields of knowledge). An extension of this model can be developed by bringing in other systems ideas that have been unfolding for some time in non-US geographical contexts, including AST in the UK.

The dialogue is represented through my own personal conceptual and practical journey. I first study the history of creativity and the systems model and propose enquiring systems to support creators in dealing with emerging tensions. I then present insights and reflections on the use of these systems of enquiry, some of which shed light on how creativity and ethics could be better integrated into the lives of creators. I hope the integration of concepts, models and practice can help creators improve their understandings of themselves and the world around them, as they have done for me.

Structure of the book

The journey starts by spelling out several key ideas to understand the book (introduction) and by getting into the creativity field (chapter 1). In chapter 1, there is teasing out of how different takes on creativity have established two lineages or traditions in the field with overlaps and gaps between them, resulting in what I call a creativity 'mess'. The mess becomes a maze which could be navigated with the help of systems thinking ideas.

As mentioned earlier, the use of systems in the creativity field has given fruitful contributions in the form of systems approaches and models, enabling creators or those individuals studying them to have a wider view of their activities. Chapter 2 of the book reviews different systems approaches to creativity under the umbrella term 'socio-cultural'. In this chapter the systems model of creativity of Csikszentmihalyi is presented and critically reviewed in relation to how it could help creators identify and manage the different tensions or contradictions that can arise when we de-centre creativity from its expected goal of success.

From my own understanding of systems thinking and more specifically from AST, I then draw 'other' systems ideas which could then help creators or those studying them enrich the model of creativity presented earlier. In chapter 3 of the book some of these are presented and discussed. An initial system of enquiry to help creators deal with encountered tensions is offered.

Nevertheless, even if creators value the systemic nature of creativity as a system that is composed of several interacting parts (creators included), there is still the question of how they deal with the complexities derived from living in an era when knowledge and its protection are vital. Chapter 4 of this book presents a systems perspective of the unfolding of knowledge within universities. This perspective is based on Andrew Abbott's sociology of knowledge (1988, 2001, 2004, 2005). With it, ideas about how to make creativity more systemic (in other words following possibilities derived from conceiving it as a system) are grounded in what systems of knowledge generation could allow creators to do. I draw two strategies that could help creators advance their ideas: heuristic borrowing and awareness. With these, an enriched or extended enquiry system is proposed.

Chapter 5 of the book presents a self-ethnography in which the systems ideas proposed are put into practice via the enriched enquiry system. A creative project on the use of information technology to improve employability in people suffering from mild anxiety and depression becomes a vehicle of reflection. Alongside it, like a critical companion (think of Sancho of *Don Quixote*), I embarked on a journey of improving my own well-being. Two creativities then became linked to each other and in need of being 'balanced'. The chapter ends with reflections on how achieving such balance became an individual responsibility despite claims that the systems model of creativity shifts from the individual to her environments when it comes to understanding how creativity happens.

If we are to consider creativity as a systems capability/effort, whose responsibility is it to make creativity happen for the benefit of all involved? Grounding creativity ideas in how knowledge unfolds (Chapter 4) and in individual/collective interactions (Chapter 3) can still leave us with the aforementioned question. Several assumptions that include how creators see themselves and how they think and act could be unearthed. Chapter 6 takes a slightly different direction. It reviews the ideas of Foucault's governmentality to broaden our horizons about creativity and to link it with the management of human conduct in any activity of daily life. The chapter addresses the issue of doing the right thing in creativity from a critical perspective. It provides an analytical framework to complement the use of systems of enquiry and to bring ethics to the fore.

Chapter 7 then develops an ethic for creative living which could be used by creators to reconnect with ourselves, and, by doing so, to integrate creativity more fully into our lives. Chapter 8 takes stock of the journey and suggests ways to continue dialoguing between systems thinking, creativity and other areas and disciplines (including mental health).

The flow of chapters is illustrated by the following systems map.

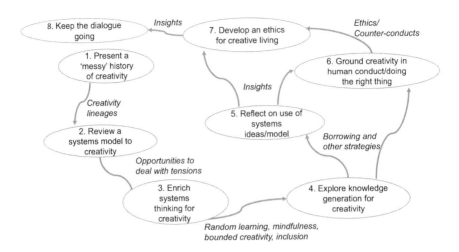

Figure I.1 A map of the book

This book in four clues

'Count Zero' is a character in William Gibson's novels. He is an intrepid young boy who becomes obsessed with finding and understanding a 'soul' that he first comes across when diving in cyberspace using an 'archaic' device. Using an analogy with Count Zero, I see myself as someone who has ventured into a new field (creativity) using a device (systems thinking).

As the reader will see throughout the book, systems thinking ideas can be used to explore the field of creativity and enhance it. Socio-cultural approaches to creativity see this phenomenon as being the by-product not only of individuals, but of their culture, values and surroundings of their time. There is scope to complement existing systems models with 'other' ideas and help creators make better sense of their journeys during our lifetime. The following are some clues that explain the book in a nutshell.

A first clue is a set of ideas to help creators reconnect with their surroundings. Some of these ideas stem from a broader exploration of systems thinking. Other ideas have just emerged during my own journey as a creator. In either case, they could offer valuable insights and reflections to manage, if not survive, our attempts to be more creative in our lives.

The second clue is that the aforementioned ideas could be assembled into *systems of enquiry* so that they can help creators identify elements (values, norms, activities and constraints) and relations between them which could influence as well as be influenced by our activities.

A third clue is that pursuing creativity could be an effort to fit within the social dynamics of knowledge. Analysis of such dynamics could help creators expand on their possibilities to borrow ideas from other groups or disciplines. This could then have opportunities as well as implications.

A final clue, one which can be found only by reading throughout the book, is that surviving creativity using systems thinking would paradoxically need us as creators to focus on the *present moment* of our creativities to make our lives ethically and more systemically creative.

1 A history of creativity

The journey starts here.

> *Utopias* afford consolation; although they have no real locality there is nevertheless a fantastic, untroubled region in which they are to unfold; they open up cities with vast avenues, superbly planted gardens, countries where life is easy, even though the road to them is chimerical.
>
> *Heterotopias* are disturbing, probably because they secretly undermine language, because they do make it impossible to name this *and* that, because they shatter or tangle common names, because they destroy 'syntax' in advance, and not only the syntax with which we construct sentences but also that less apparent syntax which causes words and things (next to and also opposite one another) to 'hold together'.
>
> – Michel Foucault, "The Order of Things", commentary in
> *Creators on Creating* (Barron, Montuori and Barron, 1997), p. 111

Introduction

It is valuable to provide a challenging and historical account of creativity to raise awareness of how a field of knowledge that continuously unfolds has begotten two 'lineages' of a closed system of thought and action that is often subordinated to economic imperatives. Given my background as a software developer, entrepreneur and critical systems thinker, the account will highlight some key assumptions that have contributed to it.

The chapter presents two main traditions or *lineages* in the creativity field. These lineages could help us to situate the ideas of this book. With this distinction of lineages, the chapter advances the argument that the creativity field can be usefully seen as a 'mess', with researchers and practitioners stepping on each other's toes even when claiming that they are different from each other. This idea will be taken further in later chapters to identify and validate possibilities in order to study creativity using systems thinking perspectives.

The chapter is organised as follows. A brief overview of the history of creativity is introduced. The overview is expanded via two lineages which show different orientations and contributing disciplines to creativity. There are commonalities and differences between these lineages which suggest that the field of creativity could be considered 'a mess'; in such a mess, this book aims to provide complementary systems ideas to help creators manage their journeys and ultimately themselves.

A brief overview of creativity

Up until the eighteenth century, creativity was easily confused with the idea of God as the only creator or inspiration of creative work: The idea of creativity as ex-nihilo (something derived from Godly forces) was dominant; creators had divine inspiration or were considered later as unique geniuses (Pope, 2005; Runco and Albert, 2010). To reinforce this assumption, creativity later became confounded with other human talents and characters as mentioned earlier. Talents included imagination, artistic flair and genius. As of today, a strand of activity in the creativity field still explores relationships between genetics and environmental influences in eminent individuals (Simonton, 2012).

In the late nineteenth and early twentieth centuries, the works of Darwin and Galton among other scientists provided us with a first glimpse of an interest in human creativity as resulting from both inheritance and nurturing, if not adaptation. A focal point of attention in science was human traits in relation to evolution (Sternberg, 1999). Although the notion of human creativity was still overlapping with others to some degree (i.e. imagination, intelligence), methodologically rigorous studies enabled a better identification of individual differences contributing to creativity (Galton, 1889). Scientific tests aimed to target groups of individuals with a view to identify individual traits that enabled people to overcome set challenges.

During the twentieth century, creativity as a construct and as an area of research and practice became differentiated from other constructs like intelligence, creative talent, mental illness or imagination, and bodies of knowledge like psychology, education, art or innovation. There are also some common knowledge elements that help constitute creativity as a field. These include types of cognitive thinking (convergent, divergent) (Guildford, 1950; Cropley, 2006); wider (and contestable) processes involved in creativity like preparation, incubation, elaboration and dissemination (Wallas, 1926; Lubart, 2001); and criteria to assess a creative idea or product as novel, valuable, elegant and implemented (Csikszentmihalyi and Wolfe, 2000; Cropley, 2001; Runco and Jaeger, 2012). There are also established and proven methods to assess creativity at the individual level (Barron, 1968; Csikszentmihalyi and Getzels, 1971; Torrance, 1981). These could help us know a bit more about the dimensions of an individual's personality that could help her generate valuable and potentially socially or commercially relevant ideas.

In this regard, the creativity field has also promoted a classification of different degrees according to their potential impact, ranging from 'small' creativity or 'c' to mini, potentially, and big 'C' (Csikszentmihalyi, 1996; Kaufman and Beghetto, 2009; Kozbelt, Beghetto and Runco, 2010). We now see that creativity can range from personal and unknown efforts that bring satisfaction to an individual, to larger efforts that could have a higher degree of social relevance and economic impact.

Recently and with the increasing use of technologies that can rewire brains (Eagleman, 2015), speed problem solving or become super intelligent on their own (Bostrom, 2016), the field of creativity could face new challenges related to where creativity is to reside as well as what/who else could be considered creator(s) (Pope, 2005). These challenges suggest that alongside creativity, and perhaps more than before, ethical awareness needs to become an important part of the agendas of creators.

Lineages in creativity research

At the risk of oversimplifying for now the rich landscape of creativity, in this section two different lineages or traditions in creativity are identified. The aim is to provide some initial insights into how coming up with an idea about creativity or a creative idea could fit within the current landscape of creativity research and practice, and how systems models of creativity could be further researched and enriched.

The idea of *lineages* or traditions came to me after reading the work of the sociologist Andrew Abbott (2001) and using some of his own distinctions to understand the dynamics of social science disciplines. Elsewhere, I have used these ideas to collaborate with other researchers in exploring a common interest related to identifying cycles of knowledge generation in the field of information systems (Córdoba-Pachón, Pilkington and Bernroider, 2012). In retrospect, I could say that I was paying homage to a way of doing research in this field whilst providing a creative contribution by bringing ideas from sociology and systems thinking into it. Whether paying too much or too little respect to academic conventions, I was trying to fit within what I saw were traditions or lineages of research that were valued in my new workplace.

Following Abbott (2001), lineages inherit distinctions and assumptions from disciplines. The emergence of distinctions and associations between them depends on what is conceived of as the status quo. The sequence of these elements through time can be called a *lineage*.

For creativity, a first lineage seems to inherit many features of the discipline of psychology. In it, creativity could be almost defined and assessed at least at the individual level. Scientific methods are used to that end and to promote further studies of creativity. Creativity can be conceived of as a human capacity, a set of talents or intelligences with key and distinguishable criteria to assess if not develop them (Gardner, 2011). The plethora of studies that also make use of insights of areas like neuroscience and strong relationships with education seem to suggest that creativity has become a field on its own with its origins, key tenets, methods of study and development (Sternberg, 1999; Runco and Albert, 2010).

In a second lineage, creativity might or might not be a definable or assessable capacity, as it might not only reside in creators (Amabile, 1998; Csikszentmihalyi,

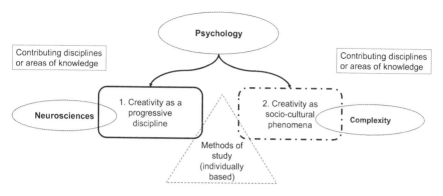

Figure 1.1 Two lineages in creativity

1988; Gruber and Wallace, 1999; Sawyer, 2006; Gardner, 2011). In this lineage, creativity emerges. It could have individual or collective manifestations. Given its context dependence, within this lineage a generalisable definition of creativity is not particularly important. What is important is how we can study it more comprehensively and how different disciplines and fields of knowledge and practice (including organisations) can foster it systemically, e.g. by working on different aspects and relationships between them.

Within the second lineage, ideas from sociology, systems thinking and complexity have helped to map and articulate the influences of and relations between several contributing parts to the emergence of creativity phenomena (Csikszentmihalyi, 1988; Montuori and Purser, 1995; Glavenau, 2010). There is a systems model proposed by Csikszentmihalyi (1988) which provides a valuable way of mapping influences and relations between different elements involved in creativity. As this book shows, there is scope to enrich this model with *other* systems ideas.

The two lineages can be represented in the following diagram, which shows some originating and contributing disciplines and a commonality between them in relation to study methods.

First lineage: progressive creativity

With the European enlightenment of the eighteenth century, an interest in the relationship between human agency and creativity emerged but later faded as enquiry into human nature and its 'progression' to human sciences took shape in the late nineteenth century. The inherited desire to disseminate scientific thinking as stemming from the work of individual 'geniuses' like Isaac Newton somehow contributed to undermining individuality. Those people who were interested in science had to somehow abide by or subordinate their individual interests to those of the scientific communities and publication outlets that were emerging. In this century creativity has become dichotomised between being scientifically and ideologically based.

Furthermore, and with the popularisation of evolution theories at the end of the nineteenth and beginning of the twentieth centuries, scientifically based creativity took off. This branch of creativity in the work of Galton (1889) inherited methods and theories to identify variations of creative traits among populations and generations of individuals. The interest to explain creativity as evolution-dependent challenged ex-nihilo and ideological views on the area. Human beings with certain inherited traits and inclinations were now seen as able to create and implement ideas. Human consciousness became an area of study for the generation of such ideas (Barron, 1972). Human creativity was starting to be conceived of as a *transformation*. Human nature became itself an accepted subject of enquiry – which principle saw itself as different from exploring phenomena like genius or imagination (Runco and Jaeger, 2012; Simonton, 2012).

With a sense of human power to create also came awareness of its potential dangers (Runco and Albert, 2010). Considering the dichotomy between scientifically and ideologically related creativity, such awareness was best seen as an ideology or series of ideologies against economic progress which required some sort of 'scientific' proof to be seriously considered. Tayloristic 'scientific' management could be regarded as well spirited although potentially misused when it came to release the human being to do other things than work. The proof of the danger seems to have come in the form of two world wars.

Some key questions driving research on creativity which transcended from the nineteenth to the twentieth century and which still drive the creativity field are (Shaheen, 2010; Runco and Jaeger, 2012):

1   What is creativity?
2   Who has creativity?
3   What are the characteristics of creative people?
4   Who should benefit from creativity?
5   Can creativity be increased through conscious effort?

The last two questions seem to have been brought by economic imperatives under democratic and educational ideologies coming from the Anglo-Saxon world, now emerging to make use of scientific thinking. These ideologies also brought the idea of creativity as a common feature in individuals, thus helping to distinguish it from others at times (e.g. genius).

The twentieth century in the Western world also saw the emergence of studies in creativity and thinking to better distinguish and understand individual capabilities and how they could be enhanced as a way of also making use of what human evolution provided (Montuori and Purser, 1995; Cain, 2012; Glavenau, 2010). As mentioned earlier, the importance of thinking for creativity was highlighted by Dewey (1910), who advocated efforts to train the human mind to think 'usefully' so as not to add to social waste or inaction. By this he meant that children's curiosity, imagination and love for experimental enquiry were very near to the attitude of 'scientific minds'. If a mind was to be trained properly to 'think', then a step-by-step, logically oriented process was to follow.

A keynote address by Guildford in 1950 introduced the importance of the study of creativity as an area of knowledge distinct from psychology. Guildford challenged the association between creativity and intelligence and advocated a focus on personality. He said:

> in a narrow sense, creativity refers to the abilities that are most characteristic of creative people ... [These abilities] determine whether the individual has the power to exhibit creative behaviour to a noteworthy degree ... the psychologist's problem is that of creative personality.
>
> (Guildford, 1950, p. 444, brackets added)

With this proposal, Guildford (1950) raised awareness about *other* dimensions than intelligence which could be related to a creative act by individuals – for example, sensitivity to problems, fluency in the generation of numbers of ideas, novelty of such ideas, synthesising ability, reorganisation and redefinition of ideas, analysis and evaluation. New dimensions required researchers to move away from using intelligence tests to measure creativity and to devise alternative tests as well as methods of investigation.

Moreover, Guildford's address was also an invitation to recognise different and more common types of creative behaviour leading to creative performance and creative results in several domains of life. Identification of individual differences could also yield insights on how to improve behaviour through practice. Guildford says:

> It is not incubation [of ideas] itself that we find of great interest. It is the nature of the [mental] processes that occur during the latent period of incubation, as well as before it and after it. It is individual differences in the efficiency of those processes that will be found important for identifying the potentially creative [individual].
>
> (Guildford, 1950, p. 451, brackets added)

Creativity as a capacity that could be developed

Moreover, as put forward by Guildford:

> Once the factors [contributing to creativity] have been established as describing the domain of creativity, we have a basis for the means of selecting [and supporting] the individuals with creative potentialities ... eventually [after economic development and automation] about the only economic value of brains left would be in the creative thinking of which they are capable ... there would still be need for human brains to operate the machines and to invent better ones.
>
> (1950, pp. 445–446, 454, brackets added)

In Guildford's view, rote learning, focus on passing tests and lack of sensitivity to other subjects apart from mathematics were not helping to discover and foster diverse types of creativity. New learning habits, educational tests and practices needed to be established, nurtured and improved. Despite Guildford's (1950) adherence to the idea of creativity as a capability that anyone could cultivate with good education, for him genetics (or nature) played a key role in making mental processes associated with creativity more 'efficient' in some individuals than in others. And creativity enhancement could/should contribute to economic development, something that we still need to live with if not achieve for the sake of creators and their societies (Barron, 1968; Robinson, 2001; Robinson and Aronica, 2015).

As the preceding figure suggests, within this lineage creativity still has a strong individual level of analysis in both its research and practice. Insights from disciplines like psychology or neuroscience about individual differences in creativity could generate changes in education to help creators and improve creativity education. There are emerging insights which suggest that in this lineage there could be room for considering systems thinking ideas.

Emerging insights from this progressive lineage

Within the academic/professional disciplines of neuropsychology, neuroscience, economics and evolutionary psychology, and using the latest technological developments in brain scanning and stimulation, there has been a renewed interest in studying how decision making is shaped by our biology as human beings (Oakley, 2014; Eagleman, 2015; Wright, 2017). Some findings strengthen perspectives that do not see the brain as a unitary information processing 'machine' with a part that acts as CEO or ultimate decision maker

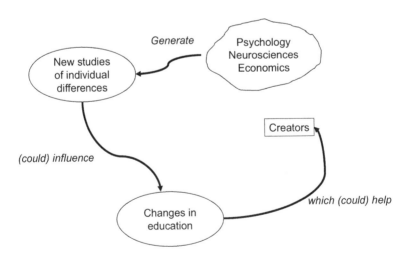

Figure 1.2 Progressive creativity

(Wright, 2017). Rather, the brain is increasingly seen as *a system* which due to its internal and competing networks (or modules) directs our attention to some things and not to others.

The brain, though, as an organism that influences our perceptions, ideas and decisions among other things is not to be fully trusted. Some scientists from these areas argue that our brains come 'prewired' to attend to primary survival and the need to pass on genes. This means that decisions are often made unconsciously in the interactions between our brains and bodies. As human beings we could become more aware of how our brains work. The more we observe ourselves the more we could understand how we come up with creative ideas; how we firm them up by not thinking about them; and how we can differentiate between and stimulate our own convergent and divergent thinking modes (Lehrer, 2012).

Moreover, contributions from neuroscience in the study of creative activity (for example, divergent thinking) suggest that there are active dynamics in the brain which recruit different brain components and networks (Takeuchi et al., 2012). With new studies of the brain, the relations between its elements when people are engaged in creativity tests are similar to those identified in individuals and relatives who have 'schizotypal' behaviour and who could experience mental health issues (Barron, 1968; Takeuchi et al., 2012). Although this finding is still being contested (Silvia and Kaufman, 2010), it could be explored further by adopting a more holistic perspective that considers how and when mental health issues and creativity co-emerge (Barron, 1968; Richards, 2006; Silvia and Kaufman, 2010).

The association between creativity and mental health was flagged up early by researchers like Frank Barron (1968) and still is an issue of contention in the creativity field (Csikszentmihalyi, 1999b; Richards, 2006; Silvia and Kaufman, 2010). Further exploration of this issue could be enriched by adopting more suitable research approaches (e.g. network-based and longitudinal) (Tang, Holzel and Posner, 2015) and other forms of promoting creativity like mindfulness (Kabat-Zinn, 2013; Williams et al., 2007). Later in this book, some of these ideas are explored further.

For the individual-based lineage of the study of creativity, it could be relevant to include mental health as an issue and consider how these two areas can be studied if not managed together rather than considering that mental health could become a separate issue in the way of creativity (Barron, 1968, 1997; Csikszentmihalyi, 1996; Sawyer, 2006). This is not to say that mental health is a required milestone in the study of creativity or that relationships between mental health and creativity are reciprocal and equivalent (Silvia and Kaufman, 2010).

Rather, this is to suggest that creators could then explore how methods to study mental health from a less individual level of analysis could help bring all different strands of thinking and action together when it comes to managing creativity. For this reason, mental health and creativity are explored together in the self-ethnography chapter of this book.

Furthermore, in advancing the individual lineage of creativity, it could then be possible, as systems researcher Francisco Varela and collaborators did in the 1990s, to bring together different strands of thought by referring to neuroscientific and Buddhist thinking to help us work on establishing a better relationship with our minds, our bodies and ourselves (Wright, 2017). In this regard systems thinking has made some progress worth revisiting.

The work of Maturana and Varela (Maturana and Varela, 1992; Varela, Thompson and Rosch, 1993; Varela, 1999) has stressed the continuous relations between our biology and our cognition processes. Appreciating these relations from a variety of perspectives, whilst acknowledging how they modulate whilst being shaped by our histories of living, could make us realise that what we perceive as our reality is only one possible perspective among many others. The self-ethnography chapter of this book aims to contribute to clarifying how such relationships manifest themselves in my own experience as a creator aiming to balance my own well-being with an idea for a creative project.

Working on better relationships with ourselves and others could have biological as well as critical implications. If we as creators can put our perceptions in parentheses as a way of fostering mutual respect, dialogue and understanding with our fellow human beings (Ibid), we might also be able to acknowledge that there is no stable or static notion of 'ourselves' (Varela et al., 1993; Oakley, 2014; Eagleman, 2015; Wright, 2017). The neuroplasticity of our brain could be the result of evolution, where we needed to differentiate ourselves from others whilst still depending on our interactions with them for our survival and even our brain's well-being (Eagleman, 2015).

For creativity, this would mean accepting that this phenomenon does not involve individual entities but rather *processes* that involve several of them; and that could be studied by looking at *systems* in the brain, in individuals or in groups of individuals, organisations or society for that matter.

A second lineage: creativity as an emergent socio-cultural phenomenon

In scientific areas like psychology, personality-based creativity is still a dominant line of enquiry in the creativity field today as it mostly remains within the domain of psychology and its intersections with education. There are, however, emerging considerations about how individual creativity is being shaped culturally or organisationally and how individuals are only part of larger systems whose other parts contribute to the emergence of creative efforts (Barron, 1968, 1972; Csikszentmihalyi, 1996, 1998, 1999a, 1999b; Amabile, 1998; Montuori and Purser, 1995; Sawyer, 2006, 2010).

These takes on creativity are valuable in that they challenge the idea of creativity being the result of the efforts of a 'lone genius' (Montuori and Purser, 1995). They also provide a better understanding of how creativity happens. In addition, they highlight the importance of both individual and collective activities to enhance creativity and make it a meaningful and happiness-seeking process.

According to Montuori and Purser (1995), the origins of this lineage stem from the work of researchers like Barron (1968, 1972) who posited that creativity cannot be studied by isolating creators from their environments; it is also necessary to enquire into how creativity assessments are the by-product of existing social values and practices. These assessments often focus on 'normal' individuals, excluding others (e.g. those with mental health conditions). Individuals' histories of coping with environmental circumstances are key in better understanding how individuals make meaning out of their lives and hence how what we regard as their creativity is a manifestation of it (Barron, 1968).

In this regard, Barron (1972) says:

> If we are to understand Man, the microcosm, we must understand him in relation to the cosmic matrix out of which his being emerged and in which his existence is immersed . . . A genuine unification of philosophy, art, physics, biology and the social sciences is necessary to do justice to the enterprise here suggested.
>
> (pp. 95–113)

With this quote, Barron hints at the possibility of creativity being also an inter-disciplinary field that could then explore human consciousness as an emergent phenomenon whose unfolding is inter-connected with processes in the universe and whose products, as well as media, include symbols and abstract conceptions like religion.

This is a similar claim to that raised by Gregory Bateson (1972) when he proposed a notion of *mind* to account for material and non-material entities that are related through communication processes of differentiation and integration. They are based on identifying, communicating and acting on *perceived differences*. Human beings use randomness to draw patterns of thought and action to adapt. These patterns can also be regarded by other human beings as 'creativity'.

The socio-cultural lineage to creativity pays explicit attention to the elements, relationships and conditions that could enable creativity or inhibit it from flourishing. Researchers have studied different settings ranging from groups of creators (i.e. artists) to groupings and organisations. Research in organisations has also explored the interplay between individual inner traits (motivation, inner life) and external factors (work, expertise, skills) (Amabile, 1998). Between researchers, there are differences in relation to if/how they consider external factors as environmental constraints or integral elements of creativity systems (Amabile, 1998; Sawyer, 2006; Glavenau, 2010; Gardner, 2011).

The work and illustrations of Gruber and Wallace (1999); Amabile (1998); and Csikszentmihalyi (1988) grounded socio-cultural features of creativity in *systems ideas or models*, by identifying relevant elements and relations between them whose interaction could cause creativity to emerge. In particular, Csikszentmihalyi's (1988, 1996, 1999a, 1999b) systems model aims to put creativity as within and beyond individuals. In his model of creativity, creators can be better seen as the medium and outcome of ways of knowing (domains of knowledge) and assessing knowledge contributions (fields of knowledge) that relate together in the form of *memes* or symbols.

As with ideas on evolution (differentiation and integration, for example), creators contribute to the selection of memes by domains and fields of knowledge which are then passed on to the next generation of creators to be learned, updated or discarded according to what society considers relevant at the time (Csikszentmihalyi and Wolfe, 2000).

Complexity in creativity

In relation to Csikszentmihalyi's systems model and work (1996, 1988, 1999a), Montouri and others (Montuori and Purser, 1995; Montuori, 2011, 2012, 2017; Routledge et al., 2008) focus on studying how creators could become less self-centred and manage if not reconcile internal or external *contradictions or tensions* emerging from their activities.

This feature of creativity as emerging from contradiction can be reinforced by considering that, as presented in the previous chapter, some domains of creativity are associated with some domains of mental conditions (Barron, 1968; Silvia and Kaufman, 2010), and that the field of creativity has been strongly influenced by evolutionary ideas that are now being taken up by the field of complexity theory (Kaufmann, 1995; Stacey, 1996).

For Montuori (2011), creativity phenomena can be best understood as unstable if not continuously operating at the 'edge of chaos', emerging between *integration and differentiation processes* that foster continuous disassembling and reassembling of ideas in the form of 'memes' (Csikszentmihalyi, 1988). Montuori sees creativity as emerging from interactions between creators and others. These interactions, though, cannot be fully planned, designed or accounted for.

For example, what could appear as a casual encounter between a creator and a potential sponsor could end up being a milestone that defines the creator's career. In retrospect, creators could then consider this insight as a manifestation of serendipity but also of the complexity and unpredictability that surrounds human beings, more so in the current epoch.

If events are out of our own control in creativity, what is stopping us as creators from trying to transform not only ourselves but our surroundings? Montuori (2012) asks. We could then become more open, humble and mindful to let our creativity unfold in ways that we might not initially envisage. Creators could consider ourselves as being part of complex systems which are in continuous unfolding and co-creation.

Moreover, we could bear in mind properties of complex systems like living at the edge of chaos, co-evolution, self-organisation or continuous learning/action to guide our creative thinking and action (Stacey, 1996). This could help creators to better understand how, in their attempts to exert full control over their creativity, there could be beneficial as well as not so beneficial patterns of thinking and interaction. The resulting sense of acceptance and awe in the face of larger phenomena as mentioned earlier in this chapter could lead us to ask ourselves what we are doing with our creativity or creativities that could link our knowing with our practicing with others.

The adding of complexity to creativity assumes that the level of analysis is that of communities or groups (Montuori, 2011, 2012; Sawyer, 2006, 2010); this would then take for granted how individuals are able to deal with tensions or contradictions. This and other assumptions would need to be reviewed. Doing so would also require challenging how responsibility for success or failure, and dealing with such contradictions, is attributed in the face of differentiation and integration activities.

Creativity researchers and managers would need to ask themselves *how far* they are effectively going by including ideas from complexity, and if they consider *other 'systems'* of activity influencing or being influenced by elements of the systems models that are being used to understand creativity.

Within this socio-cultural and systems model-based tradition of creativity research, the inclusion of *other systems ideas* could better account for further complexities that creators currently face and that Csikszentmihalyi's model could embrace more fully, including those related to creators failing to succeed in other areas, e.g. mental health or well-being (Barron, 1968; Hanson, 2013). These complexities also arise when creators want to step aside from pursuing 'evident' goals (e.g. success). As will be presented later in the book, other systems ideas including the notion of a system as an *enquiring device* and strategies like *heuristic borrowing* could also help creators to better understand and manage perceived tensions or contradictions within and beyond our environments, fields or domains of knowledge where we want to advance our creativities.

A creativity 'mess'

The aforementioned lineages could have several commonalities. Firstly, as focused on a construct of a phenomenon, both lineages aim to progress creativity knowledge. They could conceive themselves or be conceived as part of an overall scientific enterprise aiming at advancing if not accumulating this type of knowledge.

Secondly, evolutionary ideas still pervade the study of creativity. Emerging trends in the progressive lineage show that, with new insights about the brain and behavioural psychology, creative processes are still rooted in what our biology as human beings allows us. The socio-cultural lineage conceives of these processes as contributing to selecting, adapting and passing on 'memes' as mentioned earlier.

Thirdly, both lineages focus on either 'nature or nurture' creativity factors (Guildford, 1950), making the boundaries of what or who constitutes creativity often blurred. The socio-cultural lineage establishes an explicit connection between individuals and their environments and concedes equal importance to both. The progressive one adopts a context-sensitive distinction to privilege whilst differentiating individually from collectively oriented theories or schools of thought in creativity (Sternberg and Lubbart, 1992; Kozbelt, Beghetto and Runco, 2010).

Lastly, despite claiming these different points of foci for enquiry, both lineages return to accounts of eminent individuals to ground their claims about the influence of genetic, psychological or socio-cultural factors impinging on creativity (Hanson, 2013). Based on these insights, the lineages also acknowledge that there could be different scopes for creativity (little, mini, big 'C'), making creativity constructs or phenomena accessible to and usable by wider populations to foster economic growth or well-being.

The features, differences and commonalities between lineages could lead us to consider that there are no clear-cut divisions in the creativity field, and that despite some individual or collective orientations, the identified lineages end up crossing to each other's 'territory' and contributing to make a mess of the field.

Moreover, there could also be continuous 'swapping' in the foci of analysis of creativity. With the inclusion of other disciplines (e.g. neurosciences, economics, sociology and innovation, among others), it could well be that more is to be gained by looking at creators and creativity situations with different lenses.

It was mentioned earlier that neurosciences are now looking at the systemic nature of brains and how creativity thinking could be seen as collective *thinkings and actings*. On the converse, the work of the sociologist Andrew Abbott (to be explored in detail later) uses the dynamics of social science knowledge to nurture individual and group creativity when it comes to generating and pursuing ideas. In addition, evolutionary and Buddhist ideas are now being rediscovered

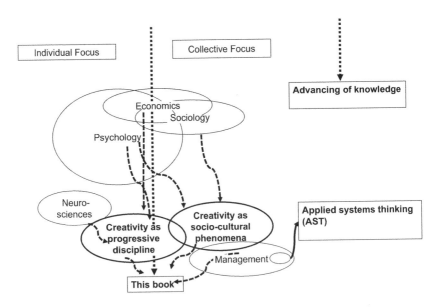

Figure 1.3 A current 'mess' for creativity

and used to help individuals manage their emotions, feelings and thoughts to help them reconnect with others and the world around them (Watts, 1951; Maturana and Varela, 1992; Varela et al., 1993; Wright, 2017).

These and other examples suggest that there could be convergence between individually and collectively oriented ways to study creativity, and that the use of systems ideas and models could be a way of bringing these together.

The following figure illustrates the resulting and beneficial 'mess' in creativity.

As this figure suggests this book makes use of ideas of critical or applied systems thinking (AST), a set of ideas and methodologies within the discipline of management that could help people improve situations (Jackson, 2003; Midgley, 2000) to enrich the second lineage presented earlier. Using AST, a gradual and critical inclusion of systems ideas throughout this book's chapters could help the reader build her own 'system' of creativity thinking and action.

Concluding remarks

This chapter has provided an overview of the field of creativity that could help creators better understand where they could position themselves. The overview has distinguished two lineages or traditions in the study of creativity: one that sees creativity as a progressive discipline and another that sees it as emergent, systemic, socio-culturally oriented phenomena.

Both lineages offer features of importance for the study of creativity in the future. The socio-cultural lineage has made explicit use of systems thinking ideas with regards to elements and relations between them which could help creativity emerge. The next chapter continues and complements the review of this one by looking in more depth at the socio-cultural lineage of creativity and its systems model.

2   Socio-cultural creativity

> History proves that great inventions are never, and great discoveries sel-
> dom, the work of any one mind. Every great invention is either an
> aggregate or minor invention, or the final step in the progression.
>
> – Mel Rhodes (1961), p. 306

Introduction

The previous chapter has presented a history of creativity where both individuals and their environments have been considered essential. In the creativity
'mess' that was thus described, however, there is still a dominance of individual perspectives that study and promote creativity as an individual capability.
Prominent individuals are still the source of data about creativity in the form of
interviews, life stories, tests or experiments.

The ideas of evolution still pervade the field of creativity in many and often
unexpected ways. Emerging disciplines like behavioural economics, evolutionary psychology and neuroscience are among those that have inherited this
focus on the individual to progress our understanding of creativity. In more
mainstream areas of psychology this dominance is reinforced by prevailing values of 'genius', 'eminence' and their biological/genetic roots (Simonton, 2011,
2012).

The historical review of creativity undertaken in the previous chapter has
highlighted how a long-standing myth about creative individuals has been
challenged in favour of a more socio-cultural perspective in which individuals and their environment interact in creativity (Csikszentmihalyi, 1988, 1996;
Montuori and Purser, 1995; Glavenau, 2010). The socio-cultural perspective on
creativity has brought about a *systems-based model of creativity* in which different
elements (individuals, fields and domains) and their relations contribute or not
to making it happen (aqui Cziksentmihalyi, 1996; Sawyer, 2006; Gardner, 2011).

This systems-based model of Csikszentmihalyi (1988) has been taken forward
to creativity analysis in groups and collaborations (Sawyer, 2006; Gardner, 2011).
Perhaps unintendedly, a consequence of this is that creativity has become associated with 'innovation' (Sawyer, 2006). Creativity has become thus understood

in terms of interactions between groups, partnerships, clusters or similar group-ings as key contributors to creativity and innovation in organisations.

This shows that there is potential for exploring new avenues using systems thinking to manage creativity. The orientation of this book is based on the pos-sibility that existing systems models for creativity could be enriched by looking at how their constituting elements could be *systems themselves*, and how the use of systems ideas could help creators and managers to deal with the emerging tensions and dilemmas that inevitably arise in the pursuit of creative ideas.

In this chapter, the socio-cultural systems model of creativity (Csikszentmi-halyi, 1988, 1996, 1999a; Montuori and Purser, 1995; Sawyer, 2006; Gardner, 2011) is explored in detail. In undertaking this exploration, it is important to acknowledge that some of this model's key assumptions could lead us to ask ourselves what we mean by creativity. Rather than focusing on creativity as the final output or emergent property of the model, we could consider creativity to include issues and processes that might not be directly related to such output, even if this means including 'failure', 'shit' or 'goal shifting' as part of creativity (Hanson, 2013; Manson, 2016).

In doing so, it becomes essential to acknowledge the value of providing ways for creators to deal with tensions, whilst challenging assumptions about whose sole responsibility it is to do it.

This chapter is structured as follows. The idea of a lone genius in creativity is revisited and challenged on different grounds from those laid out by Mon-tuori and Purser (1995, original coiners of the term). An initial and inclusive view of creativity as a system is proposed. This view becomes the background for reviewing three different takes on creativity which share some common assumptions about it being a socio-cultural phenomenon. These takes are:

1   The evolving systems approach (Gruber and Wallace, 1999)
2   Creativity in organisations developed by Amabile (1998; Amabile and Kramer, 2011)
3   The systems model of creativity (Csikszentmihalyi, 1988, 1996, 1999a; Montuori and Purser, 1995; Sawyer, 2006; Gardner, 2011)

Common features and differences are noted, and some criticisms raised in the light of the possibility of broadening boundaries about what creators think and do in the face of tensions, contradictions or dilemmas.

The lone genius: the importance of 'other' people and 'other' issues

The historical review of creativity has shown that differences between vari-ous schools of creativity thinking reside mainly on where they draw a *bound-ary* between a creative subject (brains, minds, individuals or groups) and what can be considered their surroundings or environment(s). This difference partly resides on the epistemology adopted to investigate creativity phenomena, rather than on the definition adopted about creativity.

Despite the existence of so-called universal criteria to assess features of a creative effort (novel and valuable) (Runco and Jaeger, 2012, also implementable according to Csikszentmihalyi, 1988), a universal definition of creativity is still elusive in this field (Pope, 2005). Attempts to study creativity could be better conceived of as focusing on *how* to develop, assess or practice it rather than define it.

Within this line of thought, though, the study of creativity processes is often dominated by the idea of a creator as a lone genius or an eminence (Montuori and Purser, 1995; Hanson, 2013). This idea disregards the contributions of 'others', with whom a genius has interacted by drawing on their knowledge, following their steps or simply disagreeing with them (Montuori and Purser, 1995).

In the management field the lone genius myth seems to be reinforced by adopting the notion of a successful manager who can bring about innovation and positive change to her organisation. Other people could have been as instrumental as the manager herself in the process; nevertheless, reward and recognition systems privilege the individual figure: the football coach, the inventor, the president of a country, the good father/mother, etc.

Moreover, the myth could contribute to reinforcing confusion between being a successful leader or being a successful creator, which adds to the confusion of considering that 'good' thinking is often associated with loudness or action leading to a successful outcome (Cain, 2012; Rose, 2013). With this limited view, the lone creator thus becomes action and success driven, battler, multitasker, change agent, individual, someone with little time to reflect, take a step back or even rethink her future.

Is that the main role model that creators are to have?
What if they do not fit into this mould?

Speaking from a variety of perspectives Dobelli (2013) and others (Rose, 2014; Gilbert, 2015; Manson, 2016) have started to challenge these ideas. Creative thinking could also come from introverted action (Cain, 2012), from accepting and welcoming failure (Dobelli, 2013), from spending time in solitude or from switching to a more relaxed and diffused mode of thinking (Lehrer, 2012; Oakley, 2014; Rose, 2014). It also comes from accepting problems as an essential part of life (Manson, 2016) and recognising that our world does not really care much about our own human needs (Csikszentmihalyi, 1996; Puett and Gross-Loh, 2016).

For these authors, a creative life is not one that is pain free. Instead, it is a life where *pain* needs to be chosen rather than avoided. Pain could help us to go back to our own values as human beings and to the ways by which we measure ourselves, to rethink our priorities and ultimately 'do something' even if we were not previously motivated (Gilbert, 2015; Manson, 2016).

As creators, we just need to choose what sort of '*shit sandwich*' we are willing to eat, or in other words decide and commit to a set of problems and values we want to have and not avoid, whilst choosing not to give 'a fuck' about other problems and their underlying values (Manson, 2016, original terms). In this way, creators' responsibility becomes less of a burden for ourselves and others and more of a conscious effort to be grounded and in tune with the world around us as it is.

To those people seeking to enrich their creativity, Dobelli (2013) provides another challenging if not sobering encouragement: *Visit the cemeteries!* This could refer to all those creators who wrongly think that they will be the ones surviving or succeeding. The insights of others who have previously failed could be equally as valuable as those of the individuals who get invited to speak in business and management schools about how they made it to the top.

This suggests not only that those people who are deemed 'successful' could include their stories of failures (a phenomenon that is fuelled by celebrities' stories in social media about health problems), but also that 'heroism' and the realisation of our biological 'creatureliness' (Becker, 1973) could be an essential part of how we conceive of and develop our creative projects.

Knowledge in the form of statistics about 'others' or 'cemeteries' could help creators become more aware of chances of success or failure. But ultimately our creative efforts should be grounded in what we want to do with life before we die. And that could mean dispelling or challenging some 'illusions'. This issue will be further explored in a later chapter of this book.

In addition to the insights of both successful and unsuccessful creators, as well as the unavoidability of having to eat some 'shit sandwiches' whilst we create something, we also need to acknowledge that, in any case, elements of 'chance' or serendipity play a role and should also be considered as part of creativity. We might not fully understand as creators what goes on. But rather than sweeping these elements aside when we succeed, or considering them as culprits when we fail, we could include them as part of our creativity system.

Therefore, and with an enhanced view of success, failure, 'shit' and serendipity, creativity could then be considered as a *system of activity* for creators which could help us connect with complex and continuously evolving situations (Csikszentmihalyi, 1988; Horan, 2011; Montuori and Purser, 1995; Montuori, 2012; Stacey, 1996).

From this, the idea that 'lady luck favours those who try' (Oakley, 2014) could be enhanced. Hard work on doing things right could also be complemented with reflecting on doing the right things (Ackoff, 1978, 1981) and then being able to let go of what we do not really know (Watts, 1951; Horan, 2011). As will be seen later in the book, letting go could also mean working on the 'I' of ourselves as human and living beings.

With the aforementioned ideas, *an inclusive system of creativity* could be proposed as follows. Having this view in mind could help us appreciate the different approaches to creativity that have incorporated systems thinking ideas so far.

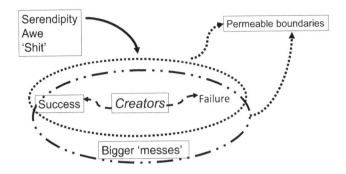

Figure 2.1 Creators living in bigger 'messes'

As the figure also shows, adopting *permeable boundaries* to study creativity could help creators and managers better understand how their interactions can be better ascertained if not reflected upon, and with a view to do, manage and not fully control what goes on with ourselves and others in messy situations. This could also help us include being open to other systems ideas or methods.

In the next sections of this chapter some of the systems approaches to creativity are explored in detail. Short criticisms are included in each section, and a general critique of the systems model of creativity is made at the end of the chapter.

Early roots of socio-cultural (systems) perspectives to creativity

In the unfolding of creativity as a field of knowledge, there have been systems considerations aiming at highlighting the inter-dependence between creators and their surroundings. Guildford (1950) acknowledged that creative behaviour could be usually brought about by a combination of "hereditary determination and environmental determination" (p. 444).

A paper by Stein in 1953 highlighted two criteria to evaluate creativity. He says that creative work:

> is a *novel* work that is accepted as tenable or useful or satisfying by *a group* in some point in time ... The creative individual might be characterised as a *system* in tension sensitive to the gaps in his experience and capable of maintaining this state of affairs ... the creative individual is characterised by permeable *boundaries* that separate the self from the environment and that separate some or all of the regions within the self.
>
> (Stein, 1953, pp. 311–313, italics added)

With this quote Stein (1953) was also referring to internal and external frames of reference for the study and assessment of any creative effort by individuals.

Individuals could be seen (as Guildford initially proposed) as having some elements (intellectual, emotional) that act together (e.g. communicating effectively between some or all inner regions) whose interactions could contribute to generating, refining and disseminating creative ideas among peers or audiences.

In Stein's account, mediating between creators and their 'external' (mostly cultural) environment, traits of sensitivity and tolerance to ambiguity could help in the early stages of a creative act (preparation, incubation, inspiration) as well as in articulating their ideas and products to the wider environment. For Stein (1953) this environment is best represented by *a culture*:

> A *culture* fosters creativity to the extent that it provides an individual with the opportunity to experience its many facets ... the stage of development of a culture obviously influences the means available to the individual for creative purposes ... Just as society affects the creative process by developing individuals who cannot relax the boundaries in the internal and external regions [of their minds], so the extent to which an audience does resonate with an art product is a reflection of the extent to which they as perceivers are capable of relaxing their defences.
>
> (pp. 319, 312, italics and brackets added)

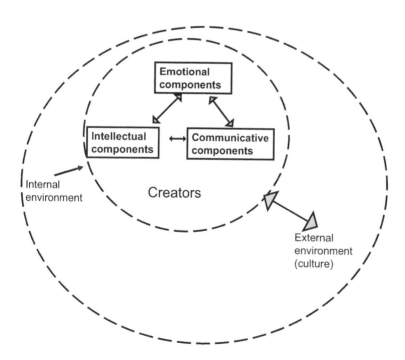

Figure 2.2 Two systems in tension for creativity

Implicit in this quote and somehow different from but like Guildford (1950), Stein (1953) advocates that the creative process could be better associated with *scientific enquiry*: Hypotheses are to be formed out of acute observation of a phenomenon, and if individuals have the abilities to tolerate ambiguity, persist and convince, hypotheses are to be tested and validated. This is like the type of thinking that Dewey (1910) envisaged to help learners deal with phenomena of knowledge fragmentation in education. Adopting a scientific approach to thinking according to Dewey could help overcome such fragmentation.

This type of thinking and acting is still very influential in many of our educational systems. It could help, but it could also constrain creativity. As will be seen later in the book, when using systems ideas to study or advance creativity, it is important to be aware of how education could become a 'mall', a stalling system to experiencing creativity in life.

Despite considering a degree of connectedness between individuals and their environments, and giving room to other domains of creativity (i.e. art), both Stein and Guildford seem to adopt a *functionally oriented view of creativity*: one in which individuals, driven by the right motivations and operating under the right conditions, could function effectively and benefit the whole of society (e.g. commercially), as if creativity could be guided by our idea of achieving equilibrium or pre-established goals (Montuori, 2011, 2012).

A decade after Guildford's (1950) seminar paper, Rhodes (1961) acknowledged the emerging diversity of the creativity field. There were now a variety of manifestations of the term 'creativity'. For Rhodes it was important to take stock of knowledge gained, and hence he postulated that all different definitions of creativity could be categorised in four different strands: those referring to the creative *person*, the mental *process*, the **product** and the **press** (cultural environment).

For Rhodes, all these strands interacted in the generation of a creative idea. This chimed well with the idea that creativity could be anyone's capability and not only a genius'. Such capability could then be nurtured for the benefit of individuals and society. Creativity continued to be an organised, functionally and linearly oriented phenomenon.

The evolving systems approach to creativity (ESA)

The aforementioned and other systems-related ideas influenced the work of Gruber and collaborators in the 1970s and 1980s, termed the evolving systems approach (ESA) (Gruber and Wallace, 1999, 2001; Stahl and Brower, 2011).

Having explored in detail how individuals like Charles Darwin developed their creative ideas, Gruber then proposed a systems perspective to account for what he called a theory of the individual. Whilst his perspective focuses on the individual creator, ESA de-centres her when accounting for how some of her ideas result from protracted and dedicated work which involves her continuous dealings or interactions with others through long periods of time.

A theory of an individual is unique. Its uniqueness and plausibility result from the dynamic unfolding of three different subsystems: *purpose, affect* and *knowledge* (Stahl and Brower, 2011). These subsystems and the relations between them change through time. These systems help constitute each other whilst maintaining their own autonomy. In a phenomenological way, some of the subsystems' constituent 'ideas' or *facets* (processes, products, values, networks of enterprises) come to the fore whilst others stay in the background, and vice-versa. Emerging mastery, meaningful repetition and creativity become connected by what goes on over time between creators' motivations (inner, extrinsic), their beliefs (shaped through time) and what they acquire or achieve (different knowledges).

With ESA, the study of creativity becomes more a study of networks of *facets* or enterprises and their unfolding connections through time. Because of this network type of approach, according to Gruber and Wallace (1999, 2001), there is no need to define a priori a focal element of creativity to be traced back (i.e. a product, an insight).

Rather than one type of element (sketch, event, facet, individual), there could be several of them resurfacing through time. In this way, sketches or any other elements involved in a creator's work could open different avenues for historical enquiry to build a 'plausible' account.

For creators like Darwin and following ESA, their achievements took different manifestations. Networks of enterprises and their noticeable facets (manifested in sketches of Darwin's work) helped him to have different purposes, acquire different skills, become driven by diverse ensembles of 'metaphors' or engage in different projects through time. In this case it can be said that there were some bare bones ideas and motivations which were shaped throughout his career, with him often taking stock after unexpected events, conversations or

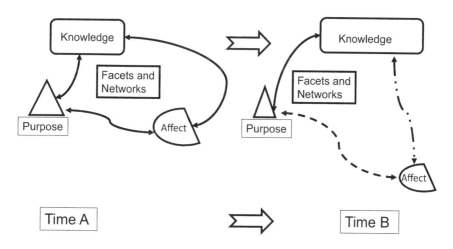

Figure 2.3 Case study of a creator using evolving systems approach (ESA)

places, which became 'occasions for growth and change'. These helped Darwin make decisions and pursue or persevere with ideas or projects in several different avenues (Gruber and Wallace, 2001, p. 346).

Following the ideas of ESA, a reconstruction of a creators' networks of efforts could help them and us realise that creativity might arise through flexible, in-depth and open if not retrospective interpretations of their work in conjunction with the work of others. This could also increase their or our degree of self-criticism of underlying motivations, beliefs, skills or values as key features of their and our creative thinking (Gruber and Wallace, 2001).

Self-criticism in ESA could be taken in two ways. Firstly, perceived failures at a specific time could be better accounted for (there were not enough motivations, purposes, efforts or networked knowledges around). Secondly, failures could be elicited to define gaps between what was going on in the background and what was perceived by 'others', leading creators to re-evaluate if not be confused about what could have been or could be the next step to follow.

In either case, responsibility to take creative efforts 'backward' or 'forward' seems still to reside in creators themselves or those studying them. This is despite the claim of Gruber and followers that ESA does not raise individualism to 'cult status', but rather that it invites considerations about the multiplex environment nature of creativity (Gruber and Wallace, 1999, 2001). Although open to considering different goals/events as part of a broader creativity enterprise or set of enterprises, in ESA responsibility to define and pursue or make sense of them is still with creators.

More could be said about taking this openness forward and in different directions and offering creators different tools to deal with emerging tensions or dilemmas. Tools could also help those researching creators' trajectories to enrich their understandings of how creators manage contradictions.

Motivation, skills and challenges for both creators and their managers

Continuing with the idea of how individuals' creativity could be mapped onto elements and relationships for research and management, Teresa Amabile and collaborators (1998; Amabile and Kramer, 2011) advocate that key creativity contributing elements arise from studying how people see themselves within organisations, and how they and their managers could use elements to generate useful and actionable business ideas.

For Amabile, the emergence of business-like creativity involves managing alignments between three personal elements: expertise, creative thinking skills and motivation. At a given time, identifying and assessing these elements and relationships between them could give creators or their managers a measure of how/why creativity as emergent phenomena could be nurtured to continue flourishing.

In the realm of organisations and according to Amabile (1998), people find themselves performing a job, often not to their liking, or not using all their expertise or creative thinking skills (mainly their ability to approach, formulate and work persistently through problems). To explain why creativity might not be emerging, Amabile suggests looking also at individuals' internal and external motivations. The former aligns with an individual's values, passions and interests and what they want to contribute to society or the world; the latter is signalled by pressures or incentives (e.g. bonuses, punishments).

Working on individuals' internal motivation is key to letting them perform at their best and sustain their ability to come up with creative ideas or solutions. This could be partially achieved by giving them freedom and autonomy so that they feel respected and valued. Inner motivation also needs to be continuously fuelled so that the work itself, rather than its products, is motivating (Amabile, 1998, p. 79; Amabile and Kramer, 2011).

Amabile and Kramer (2011) also say that motivation can affect or be affected by two additional elements: *perceptions* (what we make sense of) and *emotions* (what we bodily experience and such further categorise as pleasant or unpleasant). Together with inner motivation, they constitute an individual's *inner life*, one which aims to fulfil meaningful and higher purposes. This type of life needs to be acknowledged and nurtured. The interplay of different factors contributing to creativity at work is presented in the following diagram.

To foster creativity, Amabile and collaborators encourage managers to provide adequate working conditions for individuals to live out their inner purposes and align their motivation, expertise and skills with matched working challenges; to give them autonomy in the means to pursue agreed ends; to appropriately organise people in diverse yet cohesive teams that are driven by common interests; to provide spaces for expression of emotions and validation

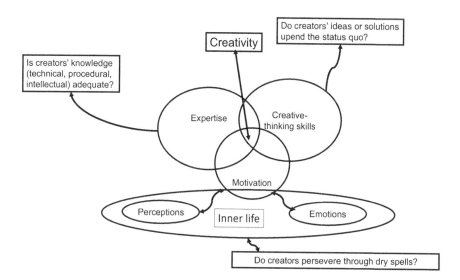

Figure 2.4 Creativity as the interplay of personal and contextual factors

of perceptions; and to receive encouragement, positive feedback and reward even after failing. In short, fostering creativity requires in the eyes of Amabile and collaborators a 'whole' cultural change.

Although Amabile identifies an interplay between creators and their audiences for creativity to happen, there is still the question of how individual or systemic her ideas are. For Glavenau (2010) the difference resides in considering working conditions as environmental factors or as important elements of a system of creativity. For him, Amabile's work leans more towards the paradigm of 'I creator', as conditions and factors are left to others (not creators) to provide. If this is the case, creators then could be continuing to operate as 'lone geniuses', unless they can work with others to positively co-own and affect their relationships with their environments.

Therefore, creators could be allowed to decide upon the goals to be met in their work, or to explore their own inner and creative lives outside work in more open and fluid ways than simply aligning their individual goals to collective ones. These or other possibilities could be considered when making the boundaries of what constitutes creativity for an individual more fluid or inclusive of elements like 'shit', failure and serendipity, as well as remaining open to going beyond organisational boundaries when enquiring about creativity.

A systems model of creativity: individuals, domains and fields of knowledge

The aforementioned systems-related views of creativity have been accommodated under the umbrellas of context-sensitive (Sternberg and Lubbart, 1992) as well as socio-cultural approaches to creativity (Sawyer, 2006; Glavenau, 2010). Since the work of Barron (1968), there has been a sense of uneasiness about regarding creativity as what results from psychological and individual tests. These tests also reveal assumptions from those assessing them in relation to what constitutes creativity. They reveal how creativity is different from intelligence, and how creators manage to deal with social and environmental pressures despite not having 'normal' upbringings (Ibid).

The focus on individuals as lone geniuses, single or homogenous entities, loses importance. Instead, there is a continuous inter-dependence or connectedness between individuals and their surroundings. Individuals as such become *entities that are part of a bigger creativity system*. Creativity becomes the result of interactions between systems parts or *entities*, with all participating entities being equally important in creative processes (M.C. Bateson, 2006).

A key representative of socio-cultural perspectives on creativity is Mihaly Csikszentmihalyi (or chick-sent-me-high, as he himself says) (1988, 1996, 1999a, 1999b). For him, creativity resides not only in creators but also in *what and how* the contexts where they operate conceive of, promote or dismiss creativity.

Csikszentmihalyi (1988, 1996) notices that through human history (mostly in which writing is present), so-called geniuses or creators were 'helped' or 'hindered' by people (related to one or several fields of knowledge) who valued their efforts, and by what was considered 'fashionable' to be or to do in society (e.g. art, theatre, science, etc.).

Moreover, creators do not build their knowledge in a vacuum. There are skills and know-how embedded in traditions (later to be called domains) which they need(ed) to master. A creative effort that is recognised as such becomes the by-product of the interplays of three different elements, as the following figure shows.

This figure represents *individuals* (what we call creators), *domains of knowledge* (abstract structures, memes or symbols used to generate and share knowledge) and *fields* (groups of specialised people or gatekeepers who oversee deciding what counts as a creative effort). For Csikszentmihalyi (1988), these elements and relationships link the individual and contextual nature of creativity. Creativity thus 'emerges' from the interactions between individuals who produce novel knowledge after gaining information from domains or being encouraged by fields which, together with domains, select what they consider is creative within cultural and social milieus in specific time-periods.

This also means that valuing of a creative idea is not immediate and might take place within or beyond the lifetime of creators. Societies acknowledge creators' efforts in relation to wider values. In short, the model suggests that *creators and audiences constitute each other*.

To arrive at this model, Csikszentmihalyi (1996) studied recognised and non-recognised creators in several fields of knowledge (some of whom were too busy living their lives creatively): artists, writers, scientists, managers, etc. Those individuals taking part in his studies often told their life stories. These are rich accounts where one can see that creators withstood challenges (wars, personal

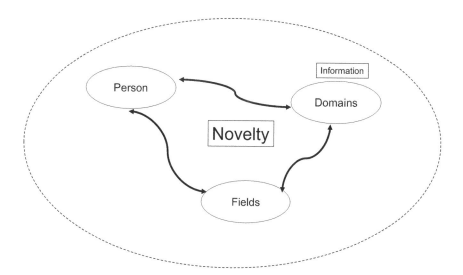

Figure 2.5 Creativity as a system (inspired by the work of Csikszentmihalyi)

tragedies like losing one of their parents at an early age, being isolated or mar-ginalised by peers, etc.).

Many of the creators being studied took advantage of or developed per-sonality traits which made them able to withstand adverse circumstances (e.g. speaking in public whilst being introverted, living with criticism, becom-ing determined whilst curious, working on their projects whilst doing other jobs, etc.). *They were able to conciliate if not manage contradictions both within their own selves and also within their surroundings.*

According to Csikszentmihalyi, what kept creators motivated in pursu-ing their ideas was among other things their immense curiosity and openness (even to challenge their own judgements), the ability to make sense of what was going on internally and externally and their commitment to contribute towards a greater and far more important enterprise than themselves or their professional realisation. Creators learned not only to internalise knowledge and criteria about what was important within their field(s) of work (Csikszentmi-halyi, 1996, 1999a, 1999b). They also learned to turn challenges into oppor-tunities and see their creative efforts and thus themselves in continuous flux. These and other attitudes enabled creators to bring apparently separate domains of knowledge together; withstand and manage criticism; and interact and persist in the face of rejections by field experts or society in general (Ibid).

In addition to creators gaining more self-knowledge (something essential to gain through creativity, which can also foster it), Csikszentmihalyi found that creators also established appropriate conditions to 'work' in so that they could experience sublime states of enjoyment and satisfaction (1996). He calls these states *flow*. They can be characterised by an overall sense of engagement with and enjoyment of the activity, in which time and other constraints or worries (e.g. success) just disappear. The activity becomes autotelic; in other words it is pursued for its own sake.

With *flow*, Csikszentmihalyi (1996) argues that creativity can be expanded to any area of daily life. Enjoyment and satisfaction can also bring with them a reinvention of the individual. Creators can then explore activities related to those initially pursued, so that they can expand their knowledge of existing or new domains. They can also establish ways of life (including how they decorate their surroundings or even their car!) which reflect their new identities.

The concept of *flow* could offer an anchoring point of analysis in the activi-ties of creators. Through self-knowledge and practice, creators could be able to find out what makes them 'tick' and when it is best for them to work on their creativity. This could open a wider perspective on what we as creators are to achieve in life, regardless of its magnitude (big 'C' or small 'c' and in-between) (Kozbelt, Beghetto and Runco, 2010). From there, creators can set up appropri-ate circumstances (for instance, work spaces or resource provision).

Flow could be a unifying element in creators' lives; its identification and cultivation could also help creators harmonise family and work relationships by focusing on what sustains them (Csikszentmihalyi, 1998). Through time, it is also essential to be able to increase the complexity of creative activities so that their level of challenge (complexity) matches that of acquired skills (Csikszent-mihalyi, 1996). Not having an appropriate match between skills and challenges could result in anxiety, passiveness or excessive relaxation if not boredom (Csik-szentmihalyi, 1996; Csikszentmihalyi and Wolfe, 2000).

As flow becomes something to gain and maintain, its pursuit requires crea-tors to establish and defend priorities to invest their time. Saying no, planning relevant goals for the next day, organising schedules and venturing to explore similar but new domains or fields of knowledge (Csikszentmihalyi, 1996) are essential to focus energy into what creators know gives them flow possibilities. By focusing on flow, creators can establish daily objectives that they know will bring them a sense of achievement and satisfaction. This can also help them avoid lapsing or relapsing into states of entropy where excessive self-rumination might drain their energy and motivation (for instance, when suffering from depression or anxiety) (Ibid).

Future research bringing knowledge from neuroscience to psychology and management could shed more insights into finding out more about how crea-tivity flow stages unfold, and how they could be better managed. Csikszent-mihalyi (1996) argues that creators need to rest when not engaged in their activities. Some recent findings suggest that the human brain needs to be in a more diffused mode of activity to create associations between apparently disparate ideas (Takeuchi et al., 2012; Oakley, 2014). From the perspective of this book, it would be important to place flow in a wider system of meaning-ful human activity of creators (Checkland, 1981) so that the management of contradictions or tensions by creators could be explored in more detail. Some key questions about flow can be formulated:

- Does flow need creators to create appropriate conditions to deal with 'fail-ure' or 'shit' if not serendipity in our lives?
- Does flow in specific creativity domains or fields contribute to enhancing creators' own well-being or the well-being of others?
- Is flow subordinated to the achievement of individual or societal goals? What about dealing with tensions or dilemmas?

A critique of the systems model of Csikszentmihalyi

For Csikszentmihalyi (1996) and followers, adopting a socio-cultural approach to creativity, mastering one or several domains of knowledge or entering or interacting with people in different knowledge fields requires continuous dedi-cation. As part of integration and differentiation processes, this also entails being able to do things that people do not normally feel comfortable with – for instance, overcoming initial fears of failure, moving on from their past achieve-ments or goals or venturing to present ideas to different audiences (Cain, 2012; Gilbert, 2015; Manson, 2016).

Given the amount of energy that human bodies and brains offer and require, as well as the satisfaction that flow could offer once it is experienced, creators would need to become more self-aware of how this energy is (to be) allocated, spent and renewed (Cain, 2012; Lehrer, 2012; Dolan, 2015). It is up to creators and educators to provide adequate ways for the former to steer clear from potential addictions, mind altering drugs, false illusions or shortcuts to achieving flow and enhancing creativity (Csikszentmihalyi, 1999b).

As mentioned before, Csikszentmihalyi (1996) has also found that creators concede equal importance to their mentoring or family relationships as well as their work. Families can provide a source of energy renewal if not a grounding into the mundanities of life that often could become unappreciated or undervalued. They can generate a good balance of *integration and differentiation* in creators (Csikszentmihalyi, 1998; Routledge et al., 2008). This means that they could provide support and grounding in productive creativity habits whilst enabling creators to become autonomous and independent to pursue their own interests via *flow*.

In this regard, however, the creativity field is divided into camps that see family harmony (via integration and differentiation as just mentioned) (Csikszentmihalyi, 1996; Routledge et al., 2008) or family dysfunctionality (Barron, 1968) as distinct but valuable sources of creativity. Whilst contradictions, differentiation and integration are integral and collectively processes of creativity phenomena according to the systems model (Csikszentmihalyi and Wolfe, 2000; Routledge et al., 2008), *responsibility of their management seems to be separately left to individual creators*, those studying them (i.e. psychologists) or those managing domains or fields of knowledge if not families or educators.

Here the systemic nature of creativity in the systems model becomes diluted. Contradictions or tensions in the face of complexity become acknowledged and valuable *but up to a point* where some *aligned* relationships with success are deemed as relevant (Hanson, 2013). The reliance on eminence or genius as a still relevant source for the study of creators could obscure a wider understanding of unintended if not emergent paths followed by less successful individuals, including those that could be regarded as leading to 'failure' (Ibid).

The already mentioned elements of failure, serendipity and 'shit' could become difficult to include in Csikszentmihalyi's systems model of creativity if the intentions of creators or those studying creativity are otherwise (Horan, 2011; Hanson, 2013). If complexity is to be accounted for, it should be considered *more widely*, so that individuals do not become goal seeking systems or rocks but rather 'birds' whose trajectories in dealing with contradictions we cannot fully determine (Chapman, 2002; Horan, 2011).

Therefore, deeper and critical reflection on the *permeable boundaries* already mentioned and adopted both by creators and by those studying them needs to take place if richer systems models of creativity are to be further identified and managed in creativity situations (Midgley, 2000).

Dealing with tensions and contradictions

How can creators therefore deal with tensions or contradictions? Csikszentmihalyi (1999b) acknowledges that the search for spaces or moments for individual flow could become addictive. People need to be taught about deciding on and managing them with the help of others. He says:

> It is not so easy, especially for young people, to tell what is truly in their interest from what will only harm them in the long run. This is why John Locke cautioned people not to mistake imaginary happiness for real happiness and why 25 centuries ago Plato wrote that the most urgent task for educators is to teach young people to find pleasure in the *right things*.
>
> (p. 827, italics added)

In an informal chat with a prominent US professor on sustainable operations management in summer 2017, I found that at some point during his academic career he moved jobs not because of the prospects of advancing his career, but because of family reasons. He was fortunate to find in his new job opportunities to continue bringing together separate domains of knowledge (operations management and sustainability in this case). This example brings to the fore the issue of how creators can manage if not reconcile – either temporarily or permanently – the different tensions that arise in and beyond the dynamics of the knowledge domains or fields in which they work.

To address this question, it becomes important to widen our understanding of how systems ideas could be used to complement systems models of creativity like Csikszentmihalyi's. Creators and those studying them would need to take a wider view of what happens or could happen when *presently* dealing with tensions or contradictions. In such situations, the systems model of creativity can be enriched to account for individuals' 'other systems', whose activities, goals, failures and 'shit' would need to be considered rather than fully determined in terms of integration, differentiation or success (Hanson, 2013).

Moreover, a wider view of tensions/contradictions in the systems model would also need to account for the *fragmented nature of domains and fields of knowledge*, as Csikszentmihalyi (1988) and collaborators (Gardner, Csikszentmihalyi and Damon, 2001) have begun to acknowledge. In line with emerging debates in the creativity field mentioned earlier, and with what chapter 4 of this book advocates, knowledge processes in creativity are not linear, homogeneous or predictable activities (Abbott, 2001; Stierand, Dorfler and MacBryde, 2014). This would also mean that other people around creators could not only support but also compete against them.

It follows that the systems model of creativity of Csikszentmihalyi and collaborators could be expanded into studying in more detail two fronts:

1   *Individuals*, to account for dealing with 'other' (life related) tensions and 'other systems' that they are part of (e.g. family, work)
2   *Domains and fields of knowledge*, whose unfolding as part of other interconnected systems could give us further insights about how knowledge unfolds in societies

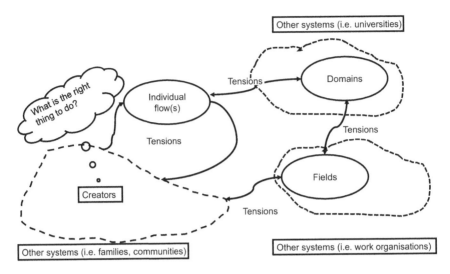

Figure 2.6 Creators, fields and domains of knowledge as being part of other systems

As the figure indicates, it becomes important to help creators to be able to ask themselves questions about *what the right things to do are at present.* Creativity could then (and should, in my view) include ethical reflection. This aspect will be further developed later in the book. For now, it suffices to say that a wider understanding of creativity is needed, one which accounts for its different features and manifestations in different contexts or environments where creators operate.

In the next two chapters of this book some ideas are presented to enrich Csikszentmihalyi's model of creativity and with a view to offer insights to enhance a systemic understanding of creativity with consideration of tensions and contradictions. In the later chapters, the issue of doing the right thing, and therefore being ethical, is then revisited and directly addressed.

Concluding remarks

This chapter has argued that systems ideas for creativity are not new whilst being valuable under a second lineage that has been highlighted for the field of creativity. In fact, these ideas constitute an important part of socio-cultural understandings of creativity.

A historical review of these ideas has suggested that creativity has always had, in lesser or greater degree, *a notion of system embedded into it*, a notion that puts emphasis on one (individuals, minds) or other parts (processes, products, values, domains, fields of knowledge, motivation, expertise, skills, emotions, facets, etc.) and the relationships between them.

The review of the systems model of creativity proposed by Csikszentmihalyi (1988) and its critique have elicited the importance of going in more depth to study its constituent elements. It has been proposed to consider the different tensions/contradictions or dilemmas that creators as human beings could encounter as part of them being engaged in other environments or 'contexts', or even aiming to achieve *flow* in creativity. These contexts could be considered as systems on their own. With a wider view of the systems model and of other systems, issues of harmonising or aligning relationships between creators and others could be valuable but not determinant on how tensions, contradictions or dilemmas are or could be dealt with. There is still the idea that creators could be better supported when thinking of doing the right things as we encounter tensions or contradictions.

The chapter has argued that more needs to be said about the use of the systems idea to help advance our understanding of creativity and creators. In the next chapter some possibilities of using other ideas in systems thinking to help creators identify and address tensions are proposed.

3 Other systems ideas to creativity

Introduction

Having explored socio-cultural perspectives on creativity and reviewed a representative systems model, this chapter proceeds to suggest *other* ideas. These ideas are *systemic* insofar as they could help creators become more aware of, and potentially deal with, the different tensions or contradictions they could encounter when managing their creativities. Their aim is to help creators *meaningfully reconnect* with their surroundings, be those internal or external to them.

Some of the systems ideas propose brief or sustained (re)connection or (re) engagement via thinking or reflection activities, whereas others would encourage creators to continuously work on their relationships with others, if not with bigger 'wholes' (the universe, life). Selected ideas follow an orientation that puts more emphasis on the 'individual' component of the systems model and links this emphasis to her interactions with others.

Also, and given my own inhabiting of a 'lineage' or 'tradition' of applied systems thinking (AST), I underpin the exploration of these ideas with a key notion to inform enquiry into how tensions could be managed. The notion of a system as an *enquiring device* could help creators to describe, reflect on *and* act upon situations they perceive as problematic or messy (Churchman, 1968; Checkland, 1981; Midgley, 2000; Jackson, 2003; Córdoba-Pachón, 2010). This notion and key AST goals (including that of exercising critical caution in enquiry) could be used to elicit and use different features of the systems ideas reviewed.

The generic elements of an enquiring system to help creators deal with tensions are: *subjects* (creators); *values* that drive our enquiry; *activities* to advance creativity in the face of tensions; and *perceived constraints* to be considered. These elements are drawn from the different systems ideas that are explored in the chapter. With these features and depending on circumstances as well as personal situations, creators could adapt their own enquiring system to help them deal with perceived tensions during their creative journeys.

The chapter finishes by acknowledging that creators' engagement with tensions or contradictions would depend on *what is possible* for them to do – in other words by specific environmental circumstances, some of which could be (re)considered as constraints. This issue provides an initial invitation for us as creators to consider what we want to get out of our creativity in harmony with what is possible to do, and what we would be prepared to redefine or change in our creative efforts according to what we consider are the right things to do. The invitation is to be further elaborated in the next chapter by looking at how creators could deal with tensions related to their engagement with fields and domains of knowledge.

'Other' systems ideas for creativity

As mentioned in the previous chapter, creativity phenomena can be considered long-term and paradoxical projects or series of projects that often escape from our control whilst we are driven to become the responsible architects of our own creativities and lives. How can we do that when we must deal with so many demands and pressures? Perhaps systems thinking can help us.

There is a vast number of literature resources on systems thinking in the form of specialised journals, edited books, monographs and the like. The selection of the following ideas obeys three main criteria: (1) To the best of my knowledge, they have not been adopted in the field of creativity, at least not explicitly; (2) they embrace the possibility of creators experiencing tensions or dilemmas; and (3) they have the potential of systems to help creators advance their thinking and action.

This latter criterion is something that neither the progressive nor socio-cultural lineages to creativity seem to have fully embraced. If they have, there could be a need to help not only creativity researchers but individuals who might like to see a wider picture of their creative efforts that includes their personal lives.

The selected systems ideas are:

1   'Beating' or redesigning systems
2   Random and inter-connected learning
3   Mindful thinking and experiencing

Each of them will be presented in the following sections together with an assessment.

Before I do so, an introduction to applied systems thinking to management (AST) and the idea of a system as an *enquiring device* for creativity is developed.

Applied systems thinking to management (AST)

Applied systems thinking to management (AST) is a body of knowledge that aims to help managers and others involved in a situation or 'mess' to articulate and synthesise diverse perspectives about it (Ackoff, 1981). Participants in a situation could identify, reflect, debate or act upon issues or possibilities to improve different aspects of such a mess. Intervention in a situation could range from reconceptualising to taking politically oriented action about it (Midgley,

2000). Such an intervention could be supported if not enhanced using critical social theories and their emphasis on issues of alienation or marginalisation due to power relations that influence the shaping of improvement agendas, policies or plans.

From developments in AST, there are several goals that can be attributed to it:

- Challenging one-size fits all and goal-oriented management approaches which often fail to clearly define the problems to be addressed (Checkland, 1981; Ackoff, 1981). In this regard, the idea of a system could be used as an enquiring device to make sense of messes and identify relevant problems or solutions and connections between them.
- Promoting reflection on the systems boundaries and value judgements adopted to define the problem and select the means, stakeholders or measures of success in a situation (Churchman, 1968; Ulrich, 1983; Midgley, 2000). The idea of a system as an enquiring device could be used to describe or problematise situations of inclusion, exclusion and marginalisation of people and issues from decision making, and explore possibilities for improvement.
- Expanding enquiry to include the perspectives of wider communities and other stakeholders whose perceptions, goals and actions are to impact and be impacted by decisions of a system under study (Ackoff, 1981; Midgley, 2000).

In AST, creativity has been considered a construct to help individuals understand a problematic situation (divergent thinking) and generate insights into what happens or how to go about solving the problem. For example, Flood and Jackson's (1991) Total Systems Intervention (TSI) approach to problem solving employs metaphors to initially help those involved in a situation elicit relevant issues, as well as support decisions about the most adequate methodology or method to tackle them. Ulrich's (1983) and Midgley's (2000) boundary critique focuses on the enquiry process and helps participants bring forth people and issues that might have been marginalised from decision making, so that reflection on values adopted and consequences can take place.

Also, Ackoff's (1978) view on creativity seems closer to nurturing divergent thinking in problem solving by challenging individuals' definitions of problems or solutions, so they do not become constrained by existing or taken for granted assumptions. What the 'problem' to 'solve' is could be challenged by revising what creators mean by these terms. A problem could become a system of problems with different decision makers, stakeholders and ideas to bring wider improvement if creators also consider that the problem could be solved (maximising outputs), resolved (satisficing outputs) or dissolved (changing values so that existing choices are no longer meaningful).

An enquiry system

Either implicitly or implicitly, these and other examples of AST approaches have adopted *the idea of a system as a device for enquiry into situations*. It was

Churchman (1968) who first highlighted how the definition of what or who constitutes a system is strongly influenced by the values of those defining it. For Churchman (a philosopher), the apparent value free judgements of planners in relation to social plans needed to be subjected to dialectical enquiry to secure resulting improvements, which could also benefit future generations (Ibid).

Following Churchman, Peter Checkland (1981) proposed that in any social intervention (one in which social affairs were central even to the design of goal-oriented systems), the very same enquiry could be *a system*. With his Soft Systems Methodology (SSM), he then provided an iterative and open-ended system to learn about if not improve a situation. In general terms, people could draw and use systems models to consider possibilities for improvement, which could then be *accommodated* according to what they consider to be systemically feasible and culturally desirable.

Churchman (1968) encouraged planners to consider other people's perspectives when securing sustainable improvements. In this line of thought, and using pictures or systems models (Checkland, 1981), creators are planners subject to debate about their ideas and supporting values. Whether this debate is explicitly articulated, or whether it is just about creators asking (themselves) questions based on their pictures or systems models about how they see the world (Checkland and Scholes, 1990), creators would need to decide on the boundaries that they want to adopt for their enquiry (Midgley, 2000).

The work of some AST researchers could be then geared to the *individual* level of enquiry where the idea of a system is used to help creators better understand themselves as well as the situations they are facing. Furthermore, creators could consider including their *human experiences* and those of others as part of their enquiries. By 'experiences' I mean comprehensive accounts of their thinking, acting or feeling which could be or not be related initially to what creators consider it important to enquire about.

To date not many AST approaches or methodologies seem to enable explicit reflection or articulation of these experiences (Córdoba-Pachón, 2011). Using the idea of a system and to deal with perceived tensions or contradictions, human experiences could be subjected by creators to a reflection on their *boundaries and associated value judgements* (Churchman, 1968; Ulrich, 1983; Midgley, 2000).

Experiences could thus be a very valuable source of information and could also help creators rethink the purposes, reflections about or orientations of their creativity. As this book aims to show, experiences could elicit tensions, contradictions or insights as well as 'other' boundaries for thinking and acting. Following Checkland (1981), boundaries could be decided upon by considering the experience of creativity or creativities *as a human activity system* (Ibid) that could be composed of the following elements and questions associated with them:

1 *Subject(s)*, creator(s) or points of foci: intra–individual (i.e. mind modules); individual; inter–individual (groups); intra-group (networks). Who are/ could be the creators?

2   *Activities* performed by creative subjects or involved in creative processes. What are we doing or could we do to deal with perceived tensions and contradictions?
3   Underlying *values* that legitimise or support our creativity as a worthwhile effort. These include creativity as a possibility for development (economic, social, personal, cultural, etc.). Why are we doing this? What values influence us as creators in our thinking and doing?
4   Perceived tensions or contradictions as *constraints* about what creators are to live with and which influence perceived tensions or dilemmas. What issues or aspects of our environments or surroundings could we not control? What issues or aspects would we need to live with?

The choice of what elements/questions and relations could constitute this enquiry system would depend on the creators' considerations when engaging with their tensions/dilemmas that are part of 'messes' as containing the whole of creators' experiences. There could be personal or environmental circumstances where some systems ideas could be more relevant and appropriate than others. *Using systems ideas, creators could also expand their experiences and potentially transform their environments* (Midgley, 2000; Montuori, 2011). Following Montuori (2011) and Ackoff (1978, 1981), because of thinking and action through experience, some of the perceived constraints of the aforementioned system could be 'removed' (or dissolved) once we as creators redefine the purposes of our enquiry and the values that we are driven by (efficiency or else).

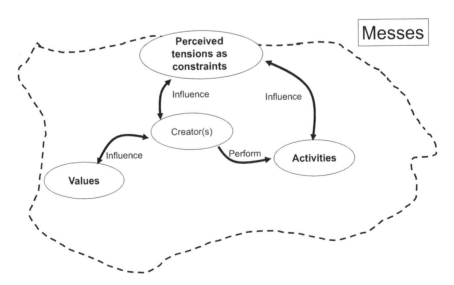

Figure 3.1 A system for enquiry into creators' tensions or contradictions

Nevertheless, and following the goals of AST, *a degree of (critical) caution* is to be exerted (Jackson, 2003; Midgley, 2000). Being systemic in AST also means considering the contexts, surroundings or *environments* where a systems intervention takes place, and being critical about them. Assessment of strengths and limitations of ideas (including that of the system of enquiry) is to be exerted when intervening in any situation (Ibid). Local ideas about improvement (what it means, how to pursue it) could be then integrated into enquiry (Midgley, 2000).

In the following sections, other systems ideas are presented. They offer different degrees of (re)*connecting* with inner and outer environments. The degree of (re)connecting ranges from brief to more sustained engagements, and in this regard these ideas consider that creativity requires sustained practice (Csikszentmihalyi, 1996; Lehrer, 2012). The literature of AST has focused on enabling somehow brief interventions or facilitations, given that its commitment to critical emancipation of those involved in a situation would suggest that they are the ones who need to be empowered to act further.

However, if enquiry has creators at the centre of it, their enquiry could then yield insights that would require us as creators to be protractedly engaged with activities as an essential part of our lives (Csikszentmihalyi, 1988). Therefore, some of these ideas are revisited later in the book to offer ethical guidance for creators to live more meaningful lives in the face of long creative journeys.

Beating or redesigning systems

Ackoff (1978) and collaborators are of the view that any improvement to a situation as a system needs to consider the wider systems which people conceive it to be part of. Improvement then involves creative thinking and acting not only within but also outside situations.

For Ackoff (1978), a problem or situation can be conceived of as a *system* in which decision makers assume certain aspects or variables to be (un)manageable and in specific ways. A situation as a system can then be redesigned by reviewing assumptions, variables and derived behaviours from stakeholders. By proposing to beat/redesign existing systems 'out there' (e.g. bureaucracies), Ackoff and Rovin (2005) encourage creators to *push* the boundaries of their enquiry to also plan improvements to influence wider systems that people are part of.

Pushing boundaries means challenging assumptions about a situation which could become difficult for decision makers to fully justify beyond their preferences or what they think is the status quo. For example, a problem of congested elevators in a building can be reviewed by considering the behaviour of those individuals waiting to use them. Rather than improving efficiency of elevators, a solution could be to change the behaviour by putting large mirrors on each floor so that those 'waiting' can behave in a different way (checking on their appearance) (Ackoff, 1978).

Table 3.1 Beating and redesigning systems

Beat/Redesign system strategy	Examples
• **Deny assumptions**: There are assumptions about what the system assumes about itself and you, as well as those about what you assume about yourself and the system. Show the system that challenging its incorrect assumptions can lead those affected by its actions (including yourself) to dissolve a problem. • **Do unto the system what it would do unto you**: Apply irrationality to the so-called rationality of a bureaucracy by showing the system how such irrationality can beat the system back and thus needs to be managed. • **Making systems unbeatable**: Design them so that they and their assumptions do not need to be challenged.	• Let a system know how long you are willing to wait for and act on it. • Not accepting the first no of a system could lead to a better chance of getting what one wants from it. • Cooperation between internal units of a system cannot be imposed and does not always benefit them. • Do not assume that unintended consequences will not occur even after careful planning. • Threaten the system as it threatens you. • Clog the system until you get a change in response. • Place responsibility for failure back onto the system. • Divide and conquer: Threaten to leave an engagement with one part of the system if another mistreats you. • For every rule in the system there should be exceptions allowed and managed by those close to where the rule could be abused. • Explain the reason behind a rule to all parties involved or affected. • Involve users and employees in decision making at different levels. • Develop a participative and interactive design for a system, considering it as part of larger systems (Ackoff, 1981).

Following this table, an example could be to *do unto a system what the system does unto you* (Ackoff and Rovin, 2005). Someone who is left waiting in a room due to inefficiencies of a service can then charge her waiting time or cancel her future service engagements. This kind of tit-for-tat action could initially trigger a shock to a system. However, it could also lead those managers in charge of it to review how their assumptions about service and their customers would need to be reviewed, and the system to be inclusively redesigned to reduce if not dissolve negative effects.

Regarding creativity, Ackoff's (1978) ideas become closer to those of Barron (1968) and somehow of Csikszentmihalyi (1996), as for him creativity requires a combination of personal talents as well as a disposition to use them in a given situation – in other words to see creativity as a system. What stands out in terms of human talents for Ackoff is that creators need to be *courageous* to follow their convictions. Furthermore, Ackoff also provides methods to help stakeholders iteratively plan and review desired improvements to situations and with a view of making such improvements systemic – in other words sustainable and beneficial for wider communities of stakeholders.

Random and inter-connected learning

Gregory and Mary Catherine Bateson (father and daughter) argue that our living with paradoxes and tensions relates to the ways we *learn* about the world. To them, Western thinking has strongly promoted the idea that learning is about abstracting and generalising as if we were all scientists aiming to discover universal laws. For these researchers, this does not reflect our condition of living beings who are in continuous interaction with our surroundings and depend on our biological condition to do so. Learning should be about coping and adaptation. Scientific activities of abstracting or generalising belong to a different logical category that has implications for our living but that should not be confused with it.

From the 1950s onwards, Gregory Bateson paved the way for an integrated view of ontology and epistemology of living beings and nature which could influence a more comprehensive understanding of creativity. In his work, key elements need to be included to provide such integration between people and the natural environment. One of them is *difference* as a kind of interface that enables *communication* to take place within self-governed systems. Such interfacing occurs only when there is a context in which communication is given differential meaning.

In other words, communication is about the difference of differences (Bateson, 1972, 1979). Living beings are somehow 'blind' to perceiving phenomena unless they can interpret them in terms of differences. Their learning and adaptation do not occur unless there are perceived differences to be acted upon. Furthermore, such differences require a *context* that gives meaning to them. A context enables entities of systems which take part in communication (people, groups, objects, living beings) to deal with potential contradictions between different logical types of information (Ibid). Some of these types refer to the entities, whereas others refer to their abstractions (M.C. Bateson, 2006).

Contextualising communication also means being able to differentiate between different logical types. It is not the same to attribute certain features to a single entity (i.e. a person) as to a whole class of the same entity (i.e. humankind). Differentiation would also suggest that symbols (e.g. a flag, a word) are different from the things they refer to (a country). For Gregory Bateson contradictions in communication arise when these differentiations are obliterated and cause confusion in the ways in which individuals are perceiving the world. Some if not many of these contradictions, called 'double binds', could be harmful for living entities (Bateson, 1972). As later explained by Mary Catherine Bateson (2006):

> We live in a chronic situation of adapting to unfamiliar ideas and new learning which creates constant dissonance with old ideas, often through

the disparity between learning at home and in school. The [learning] system proclaims the legitimacy of questioning – but only up to a point and then punishes it . . . Most schooling imposes these contradictions without being mindful that the costs involved for children are high even though the emotional stakes in school are not as high as they are at home.

(p. 18, brackets added)

To appropriately manage tensions, Gregory Bateson (1972) suggests that living entities need to be able to deal with a degree of *randomness* in their surroundings, from which they could be open to ironing out perceived differences and engaging in adaptive interactions via communication. Out of many possibilities for interpretation of differences, entities would then select those most appropriate for their survival.

Here Gregory Bateson is stating that *random exploration could precede creative thinking and acting*. This is important given that he is not stating that randomness is to be fully tolerated. Rather, it needs to be respected and filtered so that it helps 'disturb' existing communication patterns (some of which could be detrimental to adaptation) and trigger new (exploratory and creative) ones.

Moreover, for a creative entity (creator), perceived randomness would then be followed by ways to *bracket* any communication between entities as valuable and context dependent (Maturana and Varela, 1992; M.C. Bateson, 2006) – in other words as *situated whilst inter-connected*. With this type of communication being considered as a valid and necessary way of learning, creative entities could then engage in desirable patterns of interaction to help them deal with randomness. Mary Catherine Bateson (2006) says:

What we need to do is to find a way of preparing children to live at multiple [logical and often contradictory] levels [of communication] by embedding an awareness of multiple levels in our education systems . . . The ideal is to make the student able to think at multiple levels, to understand the relationship between alternative grammars where one is socially preferred, the different kinds of efficiency of different procedures, the possibility of different truths that are not contradictory because they are 'true' in different ways.

(p. 19)

The changing of level of analysis or enquiry could prove useful for some creators (e.g. getting support from a group as will be described later in the book). However, this strategy and its accompanying view of creativity as something that emerges could not be made generalisable to everyone. This could be the case if we as creators are to retain some degree of uniqueness that could also be characterised by recognising and embracing failure even when engaging with others. As the previous chapter of the book hinted at, it becomes important to consider *doing what is right* for us as creators.

In Mary Catherine Bateson's account, contradictions and tensions could be then perceived as the result of (mis)communications being performed at similar or different logical levels by entities (individuals) coming from different situations or contexts. What she is proposing is to use randomness as *a learning tool* to engage with and participate in different situations, and with a view to build creators' repertoires of adequate responses to them.

With this lens, it can be then seen that creators venturing into new domains or fields of knowledge – as the systems model of creativity portrays – are in fact having to manage a variety of communications which could also require them to assume different roles as extensions or manifestations of contextually defined 'selves'. Creators could then become observers of themselves and others. They could also learn how knowledge is meaningfully acquired and disseminated.

Moreover, if creators are to seek activities that could help them refresh their minds when not in desired states or *flow*, or to engage in similar but different activities to their main creative ones as suggested by Csikszentmihalyi (1996), randomness highlights the importance of continuous *self-observation* and learning *regardless* of how it could help achieve flow. The aim of self-observation would be to help creators avoid developing unhelpful learning patterns (e.g. getting bored) by encouraging them to continuously notice 'difference', and sustain joint performances or interactions in several and diverse contexts. For example, playing an instrument, jogging or going for a walk as ways to help the mind connect separate ideas (Csikszentmihalyi, 1996; Oakley, 2014) could *also* be opportunities for creators to observe themselves and their communications in other but equally important situations.

For Mary Catherine Bateson, creators would need to transit adequately between the 'old' and the 'new', between the 'stable' or the 'ritual' and the 'novel' or the 'fluid' (M.C. Bateson, 1994). When entering new or random interactions, (un)purposefully, creators could focus on revisiting what they already 'know' and what is 'novel', with an eye to noticing differences and working out adequate ways of coping. Creators could venture in, for instance, using parallel or divergent thinking techniques to gain new insights whilst learning or combining them with existing ways of generating novelty or being 'creative'.

Through time, creators could also try to make the strange look a bit familiar. Once this happens, more routinely designed interactions could 'kick in', so that creators' participation in fields or domains of knowledge becomes 'stable' if not 'predictable'. Creators can then make their own stories, perceptions or emotions more coherent to the specific domains or fields of knowledge they engage with. As described by Mary Catherine Bateson (1994, pp. 23, 27):

> Having made as much use as possible of the sense that everything is totally alien [i.e. when arriving in a new place], you begin to experience through increasing familiarity, the way in which everything makes sense within a new logic ... Yet it is contrast that makes learning possible ... As migration and travel increase, we are going to have to become more self-conscious and articulate about differences, and to find acceptable ways of talking about the insights gained through such friction-producing situations.
>
> (brackets added)

Overall, it can be said that the Batesons' ideas have pervaded many domains of knowledge including cybernetics, psychology, education, culture and religion. However, promoting random, situated and inter-connected learning could be going against 'neat' or established divisions or hierarchies of knowledge as well as accepted ways of separating subjects and objects in scientific enquiry. This could also go against perspectives on creativity that privilege automated generation of ideas, something that Csikszentmihalyi (1988) and adopters of the systems model of creativity have rejected.

Mary Catherine Bateson (2006) does, however, acknowledge that as human beings, we deal with transitions, randomness and contradictions in different ways and often unsuccessfully to the detriment of our own health (Barron, 1968, 1997; Csikszentmihalyi, 1996). It is worth remembering that there needs to be a degree of *caution* when employing systems ideas as proposed by applied systems thinking (AST). Inter-connected and contextualised learning might not respond to creators' own strengths and weaknesses or to the circumstances at hand.

Considering our own history of interactions, we would need to become more aware of our own reactions to random situations as well as to how we deal with them by enacting what we consider our own learning. As will be seen later in the book, this does not mean an enhancement of the lone genius idea in creativity. Rather, this could be about enabling creators to live a potentially more compassionate life, one of continuous, mindful and open engagement with others. We now turn our attention to mindfulness.

Mindful thinking and experiencing

To Ellen Langer (2014, original work in 1989), a review of how we think as human beings can be understood in two ways: mindlessness and mindfulness. Mindlessness is manifested when individuals operate in a kind of 'automatic pilot mode' – in other words using what is known about the past to deal with the present, and with little consideration about what goes on around us. Mindless operating individuals take for granted assumptions about situations as well as about themselves, and use 'old' categories to engage with perceived phenomena. Our perceptions are biased towards what we already know, what we have experienced in the past or what we want to find out. This generates pre-cognitive commitments to frameworks of interpretation which could result in undesirable if not disastrous consequences:

- *Enrique, you have changed! You were tall and well nourished, now you look so small and fragile!*
- *I am not Enrique, I am Juan.*
- *Oh, you have even changed your name as well!*

Anthony de Mello, 1994, *Despierta! (Awareness)*, p. 21

According to Langer (2014), mindlessness results because many of us have been educated in rigid ways of perceiving the world. We take assumptions, models or scientific insights as absolute and in need of continuous and rational verification. Our minds become accustomed to routine thinking in terms of known and indisputable categories.

In contrast to mindlessness, Langer's mindfulness refers to a continuous attitude of revising and recreating new thinking categories to deal with situations. Mindfulness entails among other things being open to new information, considering alternative perspectives or interpretations about what happens now and being able to accept a degree of uncertainty, lack of control and conditionality over situations (Langer, 2014). In this latter aspect being mindful according to Langer is about focusing on the *process* rather than the outcome of thinking.

With new or reviewed thinking categories or mindsets, many aspects of life could be improved. Creators could review and challenge, if not escape, rigid rules or rule-based behaviours, to free both mind and body of unnecessary as well as unhelpful constraints. This means abandoning the 'unconditional' attribution of 'true' to 'old' thinking categories (i.e. assumptions, rules or procedures) that we have been often taught since childhood (Langer, 2014; Ackoff, 1978) and which, given perceived bodily sensations, might not help us cope with the world around us.

As creators, we could feel entitled to be able to discard these categories if they do not work; we could then improvise or design joint improvisations with others (M.C. Bateson, 1994). We could also fit 'problems' or 'people' into 'new' categories or contexts (Langer, 2014). For example, we could place family fathers as 'child carers' or 'breast feeders', divorced couples as 'extended

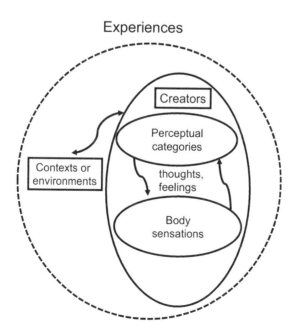

Figure 3.2 Mindful thinking and experiencing

families', elders as 'wise, passionate and still in control' people or failed creators/
entrepreneurs as 'learners' if not 'survivors' who could then work with other
creators or visit the 'cemetery' (recall the importance of the cemetery from the
previous chapter) or the 'birth clinics' of ideas/businesses.

The redefinition of thinking categories or mindsets could be a manifestation of the concept of 'flow' discussed in the previous chapter of this book, in
which individuals internalise what works/does not work (Csikszentmihalyi,
1996). Nevertheless, becoming mindful in our thinking could also help us as
creators improve *how we interact with others*. As Moldoveanu and Langer (2011)
state:

> A mindful interpretation of others' expressions involves a continuous
> search for the meaning of their sentences, rather than an early commit-
> ment to a particular image or 'psychological profile' of that person, and is
> therefore closely related to a commitment to listening as part of the ethics
> of a conversation.
>
> (p. 128)

For organisations, this could mean that creators listen to, reflect upon or redefine their purposes and operate in more helpful, experientially driven ways or
contexts than could be the case. According to Khisty (2010):

> Once organizations become aware of themselves as living systems, they
> can 'become a place for presencing of the whole'. It is then that we will
> begin to appreciate 'presence' as deep listening, of being open, beyond our
> preconceptions and historical ways of making sense.
>
> (p. 123)

This could, for example, lead organisations to ditch pre-existing ideas about
their mission or visions; to enter or abandon markets; or to cancel long-standing
and costly projects which managers still think need to be funded because they
have invested too much effort or resources in them (Dobelli, 2013).

Mindful experiencing

The aforementioned idea of mindless thinking has also been fuelled in the
Western world by a conceptual separation between mind and body. As individuals, we do not often listen to what our body or mind is telling us. Too
much emphasis on being rational without listening to our body can lead us
to "undertake actions which diminish our well-being by our definition of it"
(Moldoveanu and Langer, 2011, p. 127) – for instance, sticking to a predefined
agenda of action or set of goals, even when we do not feel healthy enough to
cope. Then, the 'fuse' blows; we give up, and have emotional and physical setbacks or breakdowns (Canthoper, 2012).

Partly in response to this, an emerging development in mindfulness is that of
cultivating awareness of our bodily experience with a view towards gaining a

more compassionate attitude and understanding of ourselves and others (Williams et al., 2012; Kabat-Zinn, 2013). This could be called *experiential* mindfulness or mindful experiencing.

The aims of this type of mindfulness are two-fold: to help us regain awareness of relationships between our minds (perceptions, thoughts) and bodies (sensations, feelings); and like the plea of Alcoholics Anonymous (AA), to work on acknowledging and reworking these relationships by accepting those which we cannot control and working on those which we can. We submit ourselves to a larger system (Bateson, 1972, 1979) and establish connections with our systems within or beyond ourselves (Wright, 2017).

Advocates of experiential mindfulness, which is slightly different from cognitive mindfulness, aim to encourage us to *notice* or pay attention to the present in non-judgmental ways using some 'props' (e.g. the breath, walking, eating, other body sensations). By doing this, individuals can then identify and take some distance from their thoughts, perceptions or sensations. With compassion at heart for themselves and others, they could then *contemplate and disown* some of these if they think that they are not right (Wright, 2017).

There could be numerous benefits accrued from engaging in short-term experiential mindfulness training programmes (Kabat Zinn, 2013; Tang et al., 2015). These include ability to reduce stress or anxiety, and enabling greater control over brain and body reactions to adverse circumstances (Ibid). However, the long-term benefits and sustained changes in individuals' behaviour still need to be more comprehensively assessed (Tang et al., 2015).

For creators, becoming more mindful of their experiences could help them to identify if not 'drop' or let go of unhelpful thoughts, habits or goals, whilst focusing on those which they deem helpful. However, this could also prove challenging. Developing the focus of attention on creativity as Csikszentmihalyi's concept of flow suggests could result in thinking and doing things in an automatic mode, which could then inhibit reflection in the face of contradictions.

My own experience of using some basic experiential mindfulness ideas with young and senior operational research (OR) practitioners in conferences during 2017 revealed some of their thoughts:

- I evoked my childhood.
- I thought: What is the problem the facilitator is getting at?
- Is this the right job and career for me?
- I could take some time during my day to stop and think.
- Mindfulness is a nice but not practical metaphor to help me in my job.
- I can/cannot bring back my mind to the present moment with ease.

This mixture of insights shows that on the one hand, experiential mindfulness could help people to be more aware of their feelings and thoughts during their day-to-day existence. On the other hand, more specific job-related needs (e.g. problem solving, quality control) would possibly need a more sustained or directed if not challenging type of mindfulness or engaging more directly with existing and specific patterns of thinking and acting. These established patterns could bring forth old thinking categories (in Langer 2014's vocabulary) and then provide a ground from which further reflection about them could take place (Ibid).

A challenge for creators who want to become more open and observant to how they think, act and/or feel would then reside in their ability to develop sustained awareness of perceptions, body sensations and feelings of what they do at work or elsewhere. As a possible way forward, the work of Francisco Varela and collaborators (1993), Varela (1999) and Wright (2017) might provide further avenues.

Varela and collaborators (1993) opened the possibility to bring together different strands of activity in what he termed 'middle' science. At the centre of enquiry is the possibility of capturing human experience comprehensively and using both subjective and non-subjective scientific methods. On the non-subjective, scientific side of experience, they advocated using techniques like brain scanning and collection of 'hard' experiential data which could be captured with the help of technologies, tests or assessments. This is perhaps what has been privileged by the progressive lineage of creativity.

On the subjective and complementary side, Varela and collaborators (Ibid) value mindful human experience as an equally relevant source of data. This experience and its validation by peers could offer further awareness of how creators' perceptions, thoughts or actions emerge from continuous and situated enactments of 'couplings' within an ever-changing world.

The integration between subjective and objective takes on experience through mindfulness has also been highlighted by Wright (2017). From scientific and Buddhist perspectives, Wright demonstrates how we as human beings have been wired to follow if not respond to 'illusions' for the sake of passing our genes to the next generation. Such illusions (mainly stemming from or related to human feelings) match well with Buddhist predicaments of human suffering derived from continuous and futile satisfaction.

As mentioned in the first chapter of this book, our brains could be better seen as biological systems whose components (modules) are in competition with each other. According to Wright (2017), both concentrated as well as insightful driven mindfulness meditation could help us as individuals become more attuned to our internal dynamics; to see feelings from a distance and decide whether to 'own them'; and to pause and enrich our engagements with ourselves and the world surrounding us.

For creators, these insights from Varela et al. and Wright would mean that perceived tensions or contradictions could be a manifestation of internal or external interactions that require enhanced acceptance of and compassionate enquiry if not reflective work on ourselves. We could use different methods to register or elicit different elements of our experience.

If using mindfulness meditation, this could give us possibilities to work on *several aspects* of our lives – in other words on how we react by thinking or doing. We could perceive novel, valuable and implementable thoughts, sensations or ideas about our creative efforts or *beyond* them. We could share them with others. We could decide to (not) own them.

However, a remaining criticism for experiential mindfulness is the amount of effort it needs to take individuals (creators) to a higher level of awareness.

In other words, it would require us as creators to likely increase our degree of engagement with mindfulness activities, which could also result in us rethinking our overall view of ourselves and the world (Dolan, 2015; Wright, 2017). Paradoxically, the very same feelings, thoughts or perceptions that could hinder creators to be more engaged with their experiences through mindfulness meditation are the ones that could need to be reflected upon, distanced from or disowned.

If mindfulness is to be sustained in the face of tensions and contradictions in creativity, it becomes important for creators to also consider an additional risk or opportunity: that of rethinking ourselves, our creativities and our views about the world. Perhaps this also suggests that, as with Buddhism, we would need to also distance ourselves from the illusions or hedonic treadmills (e.g. success, work-life balance, 'happiness') (Watts, 1951; Manson, 2016; Wright, 2017), and decide on what are the right things to pursue.

In later chapters of the book these 'illusions' are tackled from an alternative and ethically grounded perspective. For now, what could be said from my own experience as a creator is that mindfulness experiencing via individual and group meditation could help us to initially rethink our ideas or habits about our work and ourselves. From there, these could become more compassionate, humane and realistic than could be currently the case.

Concluding remarks

This chapter has selected and presented 'other' systems ideas from the systems model of creativity which could help enrich its enquiry and help creators deal with perceived dilemmas or tensions. The selection of these ideas has been made on the basis that they could help creators (re)connect with their surroundings,

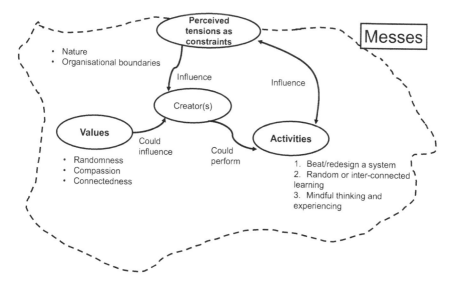

Figure 3.3 An enquiry system to help creators

so that they or the systems models of creativity that guide their efforts could be more integrated with whom they are as individuals.

Following the goals of applied systems thinking to management (AST), the presented could be within a *system of enquiry* to help creators better understand, make sense of and learn about their perceived or experienced tensions/contradictions. Putting these ideas in a system could help creators reflect on existing elements (values, subjects, activities and constraints) or introduce new and potentially meaningful ones.

Moreover, this system could be adapted by creators according to where they want to focus (on themselves, or their interactions with others); they could select and experience the different activities highlighted by systems ideas and bear in mind both values and constraints that could guide or limit their activities. The boundaries of enquiry of this system could be made permeable, as creators could then adopt a variety of values, constraints or activities that emerge throughout their efforts.

A potential and unintended consequence of the use of this enquiry system could be that creators *could also reflect* on what domains or fields of knowledge they want to enter or how they go about as part of their creative efforts. To further this reflection, it is proposed that both the field of AST and creators could also benefit from learning a bit more about how their own practices of using these ideas could unfold in relation to the dynamics of fields and domains of knowledge.

In the next chapter of this book we further enquire into dilemmas for creators when encountering others with 'creative' ideas coming from their own scientific traditions.

4   Creativity in knowledge ecologies

Introduction

The previous chapter has proposed – separately as well as in the form of a model – several ideas which could help creators identify and deal with tensions or contradictions through their creative journeys. At the end of the chapter, it was also suggested that creators could be further helped by making them more aware about how knowledge unfolds in society.

To meet this need, the work of the sociologist Andrew Abbott on ecologies is explored in the current chapter (Abbott, 1988, 2001, 2004, 2005). Some of Abbot's ideas were considered in the first chapter of this book to help us conceive of lineages of knowledge in the field of creativity. Despite not being considered by Abbott as systemic (2004), his ideas present the unfolding of knowledge in societies as self-producing according to key societal imperatives. This could help qualify features of Csikszentmihalyi's (1988) fields and domains of knowledge in his systems model of creativity. It could also help provide more detail about what Gardner, Csikszentmihalyi and Damon (2001) call 'good work' in relation to how creative individuals could still integrate their activities with ethics.

As will be seen in this chapter, Abbott provides relevant detail about knowledge and its unfolding across groups. This unfolding could help creators identify and manage our ideas by raising awareness of the importance of *convention* or standardised group assumptions about what knowledge can be generated as well as how. The system of enquiry proposed in the previous chapter can be further enriched with strategies that could help creators work with convention whilst keeping in mind our intention to do the right thing in creativity situations.

The chapter is structured as follows. An initial take on inter-disciplinary work is recounted and revisited as a key driver of creativity in the social sciences in the UK and elsewhere. A brief review of how managing tensions or contradictions could be enhanced in the systems model of creativity reminds the reader of the importance of going beyond collaborative conventions and towards 'good/ethically grounded work'. Then Abbott's take on knowledge ecologies is described. Some strategies to foster creativity within and across knowledge ecologies are proposed. These strategies are: (1) heuristic borrowing; and (2) self-awareness. The latter strategy revisits the importance of doing the right thing when thinking and acting creatively. With these strategies, an enriched enquiring system is proposed.

An early stab at inter-disciplinary and collaborative work

At the beginning of the twentieth century, there was a shift or change in researchers' mindsets about how knowledge was being generated. Knowledge generation had traditionally involved scientists working with traditional scientific methods (hypotheses testing) and seeking to generate knowledge which could be generalised across different geographical contexts (Jackson, 2003). To date this model still serves some areas of knowledge from chemistry to pharmaceuticals.

In this model of work, scientists (and why not creators) are spread across the globe and oversee different parts of the scientific endeavour. Some will be formulating hypotheses, and others designing preliminary prototypes of products; others will be testing these; and others (perhaps more managerially oriented) will be either auditing results or co-ordinating whole teams, projects or programmes. Although activities are distributed, there is a single orchestra director with a clear and shared goal in mind. The boundary between individual and collaborative work has been blurred, but mainly geographically rather than conceptually.

Social sciences (including mainstream innovation) can also participate in this model. For instance, research conducted with certain social groups can then inform general policy, which is then translated into new initiatives ranging from mental health to information technology design, implementation or adoption. Inter-disciplinary initiatives often take the form of working in groups of experts including industry or government partners. Early involvement of users helps in designing and producing services or products that are suitable for the public in general.

In contrast to this model, a 'mode 2' way of knowledge generation was proposed by Novotny, Scott and Gibbons (2003) to make knowledge dependent on its local contexts of involvement and application. Knowledge was designed, tested and disseminated 'outside' traditional laboratory settings; problems were to be first structured (defined) and then tackled locally. In this way, mode 2 opened possibilities for multi-stakeholder participation and hence for inter- and transdisciplinary participation not only in the design and generation of outputs but also in the very conception of what projects were to achieve.

This alternative mode of knowledge generation was an opportunity for systems thinkers to make their mark and promote holistic whilst collaborative enquiry and decision making (Jackson, 2003). Within this shift in understanding science and believing firmly in a mode 2 of knowledge generation, my own journey from 2004 until now has taken me to venture to work with people from disciplines or areas like knowledge management, sustainability, electronic government and public administration.

In 2004, I wanted to contribute to improving collaborative work and get a bit of funding on the way. Much in line with 'mode 2', I conceived research as a process of sharing and co-producing knowledge in specific contexts. I also assumed that any creative effort could come about as the result of adequate interaction between researchers, which to me required setting up favourable conditions to meet and discuss.

Like many others at the time, I also saw the role of information technologies as very prominent. In my dealings with researchers from these areas and from different countries, the use of tools like virtual chats, wikis and blogs offered a sense of horizontality and proximity in communication (Córdoba-Pachón, 2009). For some time, we could keep interest and ideas alive after meeting face-to-face.

An initial reflection on the successes and failures of this style of collaborative work led me to identify several challenges to it (Ibid):

• In any collaboration, there was a need to be able to work in social and task layers of interaction (Córdoba-Pachón and Robson, 2005). Non-project interactions were about enabling 'social' activity between collaborators. People could benefit by creating rapport and sharing social conversations. This could help soothe emerging tensions as well as open other collaborations. The task layer required activities for the generation of specific outputs (project bids, articles, book chapters, meetings). Often, this latter layer would take over due to an impending deadline and a need to show tangible results or money expenditure. An example of my collaboration with Nick Davey from IBM, which followed this perspective, is portrayed in the following figure. What transpired in our interactions was that despite some differences, we somehow had *similar* interests and techniques or methods to elicit knowledge:

• Related to this it was also important to acknowledge different *levels of analysis* when exploring a common phenomenon with a group of collaborators

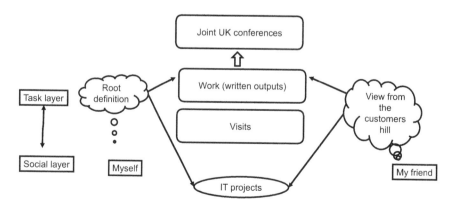

Figure 4.1 An earlier experience of collaboration

coming from different disciplines (Fuqua et al., 2004). Some of my collaborators were operating at the level of organisations or individuals, whereas others were operating at the level of policies or countries. Linked to a preferred focus of analysis there was also a preferred research approach. Some collaborators required to gather large amounts of data and analyse it quantitatively. Myself, I was (and still am!) adept at observing, talking to or working directly with research participants in eliciting or analysing qualitative data. Conceptually, I also like to draw similarities rather than differences when exploring phenomena of interest.

- Declaring allegiance to a specific body of knowledge (psychology, information systems, systems thinking, etc.) influenced the choice of theories and methods to conduct research. This also accounted for the participation of researchers/collaborators in different professional and non-professional groups, their own organisations and geographical regions of influence and their preferred research approaches or protocols. Not only was the city or country of work or university relevant here. Professional memberships, international conferences to go to, journals to target and networks of contacts also played a role in influencing what and how research was to be carried out.

Meeting these challenges also required researchers (including myself) to leave our comfort zones and become somehow participants in activities which might not be seen initially as directly valuable or beneficial. This could mean, among other things, randomly exploring different contexts to learn something new whilst using something old (chapter 3 of this book).

Since then I have persevered in keeping an open mind when it comes to interdisciplinary and collaborative work. I have become more aware that institutional and departmental forces if not personal circumstances influence what we collaborate on and how we decide to collaborate with others. I am still curious as to what these decisions have to do with what we think is the ethically right thing to do for ourselves and others, and how we frame this issue within the surroundings or environments that we are part of (work, academia, family, etc.).

As of 2018, there are *renewed* efforts to promote this type of work in the UK. Social science research councils are continuously funding inter-disciplinary projects that also have a remit to generate impact in society (whatever this means).

I am attending today an interdisciplinary event at my institution. It is about the future of artificial intelligence or AI. It is not one of my main research interests, but I want to support the organiser of the event whom I have known now for some time.

I hear about sophisticated methods to aid decision making: probabilities, simulations, machine learning, agent based modelling, use of biological and network metaphors, etc.

The organiser of this activity calls for building collective AI capability at our university, otherwise we could end up losing out . . . and AI needs to be properly governed . . . this is where people like me come into the picture, because I work at a school of management.

I have some questions after the event: Who is mostly benefiting from this event . . . the experts or the novices? Who could I work with more easily?

*Given my previous experiences, before thinking of any alignment or collaboration, I would probably need to better understand **where these guys and I come from**, and what can be realistically achieved in consideration of our individual, group or institutional circumstances.*

Beyond alignment of individuals, domains and fields of knowledge

Chapter 2 of this book provided a critique of how the systems model of creativity of Csikszentmihalyi encouraged but also limited creators' managing of tensions, dilemmas and contradictions. Whilst the model advocates a healthy degree of tension to fuel new relations between individuals, domains and fields of knowledge, it was also highlighted that 'doing the right thing' for creators could also imply accepting and accounting for failure when trying to reconcile intra-individual and inter-individual tensions (Hanson, 2013).

It could well be that – in the spirit of acknowledging serendipity, uncertainty, success and failure in creativity – there could be forces beyond creators' control that could be used productively in a given situation. Csikszentmihalyi (1996) seems to recognise this when also highlighting that in his study of eminent creators, rejection (failure in being accepted) led some of them to set up their own fields and domains of knowledge.

Moreover, failure could also account for the failure to align creators' values with those dominating domains and fields of knowledge. For Gardner et al. (2001), the study of fields like genetics and journalism can serve as good examples of the difficulties if not tensions that creators are facing when aiming to act responsibly and guided by ethical values. Often, creators find it difficult to uphold their own personal integrity in the face of pressures to make a field or domain of knowledge more profitable. The influence of (social) media in canvassing research findings can also contribute to exacerbating confusion.

However, it seems that in the systems model of creativity, it is assumed that creators acknowledge the complexity of any effort and the importance of keeping domains and fields of knowledge connected for the benefit of humankind. The fragmented nature of knowledge is acknowledged and subsumed under 'good/ethically grounded scientific practice' or 'good/ethically grounded work' (Ibid). There is a tendency to associate goodness with only one type of ethical thinking: that which considers consequences that creativity could have.

Could there be other ways to conceive of ethics in creativity more in tune with the non-alignment of complexities, tensions or contradictions that creators could be often facing?

To address this question, it becomes important to explore how knowledge fragmentation arises and is maintained in society as well as adopted by the creativity field/systems model of creativity. Doing so could help to elicit strategies for creators to work with and challenge if not 'beat' the systems that frame what is creative within them.

Knowledge ecologies

According to the sociologist Andrew Abbott (1988, 2001, 2004, 2005), Western society's quest for knowledge accumulation has resulted in the development and maintenance of social and structural configurations in societies. Knowledge becomes the result of *control* being exerted by specific groups of people over relevant tasks in specific locations (physical and organisational). This type of control ensures that only some people are 'credited' to serve the public and perform these tasks.

In Abbott's accounts (1988, 2001), groups of people become recognised professions, para-professions, academic disciplines or academic settlements. These differ in the degree of control over abstract or instrumental knowledge as well as the degree of recognition attributed to them over certain tasks. Professions and academic disciplines are attributed the generation of higher level theoretical and practical knowledge, which could then be used by other groups to make it more portable to serve audiences in more detailed or practical ways.

Academic settlements are an interesting group for Abbott (2001). They are not regarded as knowledge disciplines but have recognition inside and outside their institutional locations. They control some knowledge activities; they also play important roles in terms of research, instruction and legitimation (Abbott, 1988). Regarding this aspect of legitimation, settlements could also be supporting the exploration and renewal of knowledge by reassembling it in useful and relevant ways (Abbott, 1988, 2001).

The resulting group configurations of disciplines, settlements and others (e.g. para-professions or occupations) can be termed 'knowledge ecologies'. For Abbott (2005) a knowledge ecology is a social structure characterised by a set of actors, locations, tasks and *relations* between these (p. 1). Relations are endogenous to social interaction; they influence and are influenced by knowledge generation activities.

Relations take precedence over what they are about or who is performing them as well as where. For creators, relations could be conceived of as an 'a priori' analytical element which could help them understand how knowledge unfolds. They result from groups of people setting up and protecting if not expanding arbitrary and contingent boundaries around what they do (Abbott, 1988, 2001, 2004). A side effect of relations is that they enable some sort of *convention* to emerge regarding what knowledge can be generated or maintained, as well as how. Knowledge lineages can then be seen as maintaining some conventions whilst enabling their change to some degree through time.

For Abbott (2005), the value of conceiving knowledge activities as unfolding within and across ecologies resides in its potential to enable trans functional, trans occupational/professional or trans organisational analysis. Such types of analysis could proceed by considering how relations between groups, knowledge-related tasks and locations are maintained or change over time. Analysis could offer insights about how knowledge is formed, (re)configured and protected. It could then offer creators valuable insights into what to do to fit within convention if not challenge it as they see fit (Abbott, 2004).

Moreover, the study of specific groups in knowledge ecologies enables Abbott (2005) to claim that their success as a profession, discipline or settlement depends on not only how the group manages to retain or extend control over domains of problems/knowledge, but also how it connects with others outside a given ecology. This is the case, for example, with the medical profession. As a profession, it needs to maintain connections with academia so that its legitimacy is enhanced through research and instruction. In the latter aspect, medicine as a field of knowledge needs to be recognised or certified by professional (country, regional or worldwide) associations. Medicine has also established and still maintains connections with teaching locations but also with practitioners 'out there', some of whom help legislate what medicine should do for society.

For Abbott (at least in the US), this shows that there are relations between academic, professional and governmental groups (2005), as the following figure suggests.

Taking this view of knowledge ecology forward, 'success' and/or 'failure' in creativity could be emerging from succeeding or not in establishing and maintaining interactions between individuals *and* groups within as well as across ecologies. Abbott (2001, 2005) presents examples of how intra- and inter-ecology connection has (effectively) taken place for the case of economics and computer science as knowledge areas. Economics education in the US, he

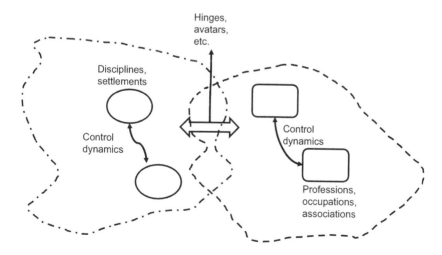

Figure 4.2 Connections between knowledge ecologies

argues, is mostly being successful by establishing a direct connection or *hinge* with government policy-making groups; these groups have adopted knowledge distinctions in the form of methods as well as forecasting to guide their activity.

Here we could say we have a case of *alignment* between fields and domains of knowledge as proposed initially by Csikszentmihalyi's (1988) systems model of creativity. In this case, alignment is being reinforced by formally established relations between groups and appears to yield direct benefits to the parties concerned (government, academia, students and staff). One could also see that alignment has more to do with *collaborating groups than collaborative institutions*. Field experts from one ecological location (e.g. industry, government) could then contribute to influence, foster or assess creativity in another (e.g. university).

Somewhat different from what Csikszentmihalyi advocates though, the alignment could go beyond organisational boundaries. In contrast to economics, Abbott (2005) argues that an academic discipline like computer science was established to help train and certify industry occupational groups. An initial set of connections of 'avatars' (representatives from industry ecologies) was set up by bringing computer experts into academia. However, continuous technological change as well as academic pressures to establish computer science as a legitimate 'academic' discipline have led to a fragmentation of initial linkages. Here established conventions for knowledge generation are continuously disrupted by technological innovations.

However, Abbott's ideas do not seem to fully endorse alignment or stability of knowledge conventions and lineages, at least not at a more detailed level of analysis. He contends that groups within and across ecologies can find themselves *competing* for controlling knowledge production. In settings like universities, the pursuit of academic knowledge is also fuelled by continuous competition and the search for 'purity', which many see as a way of gaining promotion, recognition and greater control over their work (Abbott, 1988, 2001).

Also, events like career promotions, departmental mergers and policy or regulatory changes contribute to reinforcing this. This combination of events results in continuous *cycles or paradigms of conflict, eclecticism and absorption between groups*. Abbott (2001, pp. 18, 23–25) says:

> By generational paradigm I mean a single step in a fractal cycle: an episode of conflict, defeat of one side, division of the winners, and remapping of the losers' concerns onto the equivalent descendant of the winners. [In social science] . . . The typical 'victory' of a particular side of a fractal distinction seems to last about twenty to thirty years . . . [old] ideas return under new names . . . we get to keep our best ideas whilst yet retaining our belief in perpetual, intellectual progress.

For the social sciences, this would mean that the assumption that it accumulates knowledge needs to be challenged if not replaced by that of knowledge being *rediscovered*, as presented by the following figure.

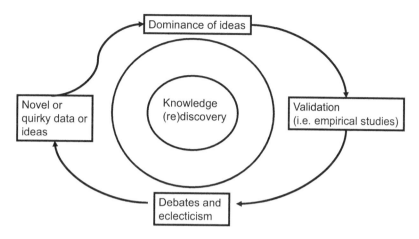

Figure 4.3 Cycles of knowledge (re)discovery

This claim would sound confusing, if not surprising, to creators who see themselves as advancing knowledge to produce novel, disruptive, valuable and implementable ideas (Csikszentmihalyi and Wolfe, 2000; Runco and Jaeger, 2012). For Abbott, this realisation could lead us to regain some of our humility if not becoming more *solidary* with our fellow human beings, who might have already been where we intend to go when generating new knowledge (Abbott, 2001). For creators, knowledge rediscovery could be a new manifestation of the features of serendipity, success or failure of creativity that were highlighted in chapter 2 of this book.

Here Abbott has arrived at a mindful value stance that could help creators reconnect with or rediscover their surroundings. Creativity becomes a way for creators to operate to rediscover or formulate ideas within existing lineages and conventions by using common assumptions and knowledge distinctions (Abbott, 2001). From this, creators could then further help develop or maintain knowledge whilst making sure that other ways of rediscovering knowledge (navigating and growing the tree) are valued and promoted.

Further implications for creativity

From the preceding discussion, there could be further implications for the study and management of creativity: Firstly, creators could make 'disparate' or 'dispersed' knowledge from different domains more accessible and portable to a variety of audiences (Abbott, 1988; Csikszentimihalyi, 1996; Sternberg and Kaufman, 2010). Creators could select which connections within and outside their domains or fields of knowledge they want to use to generate novelty. Doing so could reinforce the current importance given to collaboration in creativity (Montuori and Purser, 1995) and somehow relieve creators from having to come up with ideas on their own as 'lone' or 'alien' geniuses (Stierand et al., 2014). Technologies could support dealing with these connections.

Secondly, it has been said that ecology relations do not only unfold in consensual, harmonious or homogeneous ways. Therefore, creators could select where in relevant domains of knowledge they want to generate novelty according to how they perceive the landscape of knowledge rediscovery between domains – in other words whose knowledge ideas/methods are dominant at a time within or across their fields or domains of knowledge or interest. Creators could gain from conceiving themselves as borrowing, replacing or absorbing each other. Inter-disciplinary and collaborative work could be conceived of as contests for control that could help creators to learn more about themselves and others rather than fully achieving synergies (Abbott, 2001).

Thirdly, alignment between creators, fields and domains of knowledge could be better seen as a political phenomenon of selecting connections between these elements of the systems model of Csikszentmihalyi. In this, creators can see themselves as playing an important role. They could contribute to reinforcing existing alignments or redefining them. Political action also comes in the form of creators having to follow 'lineages' or 'convention' (Abbott, 2001, 2004), as mentioned before, if creators are to fulfil societal needs of knowledge rediscovery. As Abbott (2004) says, deciding on what action to take is not an easy task: "Damned if you do not follow convention, damned if you do".

Again, doing the right thing for creators requires further reflection on what to do about knowledge conventions and lineages.

From these implications, a refinement of Csikszentmihalyi's systems model of creativity can be proposed according to the following figure.

Rather than adding new elements to the systems model of creativity, the preceding figure qualifies some of the relations between them. By doing so, a

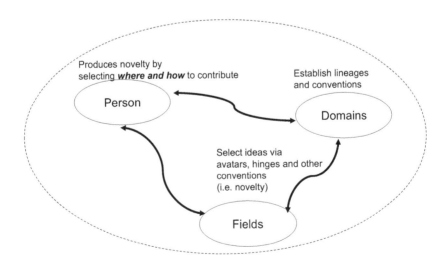

Figure 4.4 Creativity emerging from knowledge dynamics

better understanding of tensions and contradictions could also contribute to helping creators deal with them. Still drawing on Abbott's ideas, more specific strategies to proceed in the light of these tensions are presented as follows.

Heuristic borrowing

Abbott (2001, 2004) argues that at the centre of any social science effort is an explanation or series of explanations of what a phenomenon is and how to study it. Knowledge unfolding becomes a process of combining explanations. From this, it can be inferred that creativity could be about coming up with innovative ways of conceiving phenomena as well as methods to gather or analyse relevant explanations about them.

> What is universal about social science knowledge is the project of getting there [to a place we want to know] and of mutually decoding our routes [retracing how we have tried to do it] . . . once in a while . . . somebody learns enough from somebody else to wander into a whole new area . . . This process [of knowledge rediscovery] continuously creates new terms for old things . . . [*to be creative*] . . . faculty and students [could] look to fundamentally different sources and assign different meanings to any given technical term.
> (Abbott, 2001, pp. 20, 32, brackets and italics added)

Alongside mastering knowledge from one or several domains of knowledge (Csikzsentmihalyi, 1996) and in line with what could be considered *useful and rediscovery-oriented* creativity within each of them, creators could benefit by *borrowing* knowledge distinctions (Abbott, 2004, 2012). This means importing distinctions from neighbouring groups. Neighbouring groups are those who have common ancestry in their lineage – in other words they share some assumptions about how the phenomenon is to be conceived of, what level of analysis is relevant or what methods are best suited to study it (Abbott, 2012).

For Abbott (2004, 2012), key to borrowing is the possibility of *iterating heuristically* to explore different branches of a common ancestry tree that could

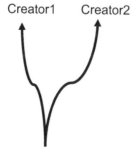

Creator1   Creator2

A common ancestry or 'tree' of knowledge

Figure 4.5 Borrowing from neighbouring groups

Table 4.1 Heuristic borrowing strategies for enhancing creativity

Type of heuristics	Description	Strategies for iteration
Search heuristic	Looking outside a phenomenon	❖ Analogies: treating a problem of X like a problem of G by foraging in other disciplines or settlements to import theory, data or methods ❖ Borrowing a method with consideration of the limitations of underlying analogies
Fractal heuristic	Looking outside discipline, sub-discipline or settlement	Borrowing a competitor's claims, theories or methods of analysis from existing debates, including: ➢ Positivism vs interpretivism ➢ Analysis vs narration ➢ Behaviourism vs culturalism ➢ Individualism vs emergentism ➢ Realism vs constructionism ➢ Contextualism vs noncontextualism ➢ Choice vs constraint ➢ Conflict and consensus ➢ Transcendent vs situated knowledge
Argument heuristic	Looking within a phenomenon: Is this 'really' true?	▪ Problematise the obvious: challenging accepted wisdom or assumptions of 'proved' research. ▪ Make a reversal: Is X causing Y or Y causing X? Explore reverse causality between X and Y to complement existing knowledge. ▪ Make a rash assumption: What if we assume something different about problem X and see how far we can go with it? ▪ Reconceptualise: Is problem X instead problem Y or problem Z?

have remained unexplored, or which have been explored elsewhere by other disciplines or settlements of social science. This could work best by considering the following:

- There is one person or several people (creators included) who are willing to enter dialogue.
- There is common knowledge ancestry between them.
- A borrowing strategy (see the following table) is used to study a phenomenon of interest.
- If needed, other distinctions or strategies might be used.

  For instance, one could import and use an ethnographic method (traditionally used to study groups) to study a whole cultural phenomenon. Insights from this borrowing could lead creators to look for generalisable knowledge, in which case another strategy could be then used.

- The preceding steps are repeated until there is a perceived set of valuable insights.

Self-awareness

With heuristic borrowing, creators could then venture to interpret a situation in diverse ways. They could interact with other individuals coming from similar albeit distinct knowledge lineages or conventions. Nevertheless, for Abbott (2004), heuristic borrowing requires those individuals using it (i.e. creators) to assume a continuous attitude of *self-awareness* in the light of the specific domains and fields of knowledge that they are engaged with.

This means that we need to listen, balance our self-confidence (not too little, not too much), aim to learn continuously, seek out appropriate mentors and avoid inappropriate ones (condescending or not interested collaborators) (Ibid). We could, Abbott (2004) continues, keep our imagination alive and renewed by thinking of the puzzles of social life that we are attracted to even in the face of uncertainty. And most of all, we need to be aware of *conventions* of the fields or domains of knowledge we want to engage with, as mentioned earlier.

Self-awareness in the face of conventions is important if our ideas are to have an audience so that they are valued and taken forward. We are to consider how our ideas (do not) 'fit' with existing lineages, their common values or conventions to generate knowledge. Often, these conventions dictate what is considered relevant and therefore worth a creative effort (Abbott, 2004).

A reflection on the 'identity' convention

Monday, 17 November 2014. Using Abbott's ideas, I organised a workshop with my academic colleagues interested in information systems. I aimed to present some borrowed ideas on disciplines, settlements and their dynamics to help me and colleagues rebuild our self-confidence after feeling excluded or side-lined from our school.

A senior visiting colleague from the US kindly agreed to support the event but as the meeting began, he insisted that rather than us seeing ourselves as a profession or settlement, we should consider seeing ourselves as a group in need of having a clear and defensible identity. Identity then became the distinction to be used to understand our situation as a group. My initial borrowing of Abbott's ideas on professions did not seem to prosper, although it helped me to synthesise knowledge.

These are the resulting reflections from the meeting which I collated together in an email to colleagues:

Dear colleagues:
Many thanks for the great discussion we had today about professional identity and what we could be doing to enhance our own (please note my own amalgamation of the terms to accommodate mine and the senior colleague's views).

Here are some points I wrote down, hopefully they will inspire you to pursue them individually or collectively as a research group.

- *Avoid self-flagellation of thinking we are not good enough.*
- *Have multiple identities to work with different groups. Having only one only reinforces silo mentality.*

- *Develop capabilities to look at our field of information systems in several areas of application.*
- *Acquire and market expertise to become recognised externally.*
- *Be careful about collaboration. Our institution needs to see more effort being put into collaboration and interdisciplinarity.*
- *Bring students with practical courses where theory and tools are combined.*
- *Be assertive, stand our ground when people ask us about our identity as a group, and defend the values we use to firm our activity and our research/teaching/engagement.*
- *Know when you have a good chance to fight and win.*

From this meeting I learned that I was assuming some conventions (i.e. needing to have an identity, following the order of seniority and accepting my colleague's take on the situation) which contributed to shape our creative efforts in this situation.

Was it the right thing for me to do to accept these? Could I have defended my stance more fiercely? What could be the consequences?

The 'novelty' convention

The preceding reflection on conventions also shows the importance for creators to reflect on or take a stance even in the face of 'novelty'. This could become an excluding way to foster creativity.

According to Chambers (2017), academic journals (representing fields of knowledge) would often focus on publishing 'positive' research results – that is "hypothesis tests that reveal statistically significant differences of associations between conditions (e.g. A is greater than B; A is related to B, vs A is the same as B; A is unrelated to B)" (Chambers, 2017, p. 3). The drive to produce this sort of novel results could occur at the expense of studies that replicate existing hypotheses.

In domains of knowledge like psychology, Chambers (2017) argues that education also contributes to misunderstanding or misusing novelty. By convention, students are often trained to always seek positive results in the form of disconfirming the null hypothesis 'H0' (which is by default not novel). Any empirical data that could lead them to reconsider H0 is discarded.

Students are thus taught that the significance of statistical results ($p < 0.05$, with p being the probability of things happening by chance) applies to accepting H1, not to accepting H0. In the future, regardless of how they contribute to advancing or replicating knowledge, these students will be better prepared to play the game of publish (as many papers that show novel results) or perish (Ibid).

Without self-awareness of convention by creators, Abbott's borrowing heuristic could be unconsciously replaced by the availability heuristic (Chambers, 2017), meaning that creators rely on our existing conventions about what constitutes novelty. This means that rather than promoting integrative, synthesising, mindful or context-sensitive thinking, gatekeepers of domains and fields of knowledge (i.e. journal editors, reviewers, funders) would then prefer to engage creators in Socratic dialogues to demonstrate their novelty at the expense of other possibilities – for instance, rediscovering knowledge.

In this way, novelty could then be confused with discovery (Chambers, 2017), and thus creativity in knowledge ecologies could become based more on probabilistic (but novel and positive) results rather than on holistic, longitudinal and replicable proofs or rejections. In the wider enterprise of knowledge unfolding in science, its building blocks could then be based on incomplete studies or in the best of cases on conceptual replications (using again novel methods) (Ibid). Publish or perish pressures can reinforce incomplete or too novel studies.

For the systems model of creativity, novelty needs to be reconsidered. The quest for it by creators and other people would need to keep an eye on what they think is the right thing to do. There could be other possibilities to develop creativity beyond aligning domains or fields of knowledge. Novelty could be challenged, even if this means managing new contradictions to help creators reconnect with their surroundings and thus contributing to rediscovering knowledge.

An enriched enquiry system

This chapter has provided a perspective on the unfolding of knowledge to help creators better understand and assess how they could interact with others and deal with emerging tensions in domains and fields of knowledge. By adopting Abbott's ideas, it becomes relevant to understand creativity as a feature emerging within inter-disciplinary or collaborative processes of knowledge

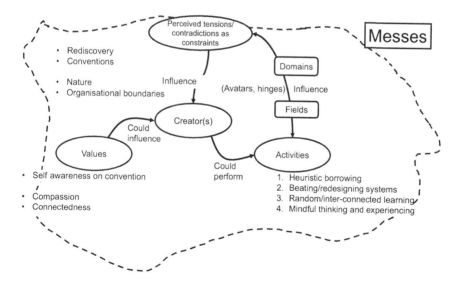

Figure 4.6 An enriched enquiry system

competition, conflict and absorption that involve groups of individuals in different locations and settings and that could be influenced by these groups' own knowledge lineages and conventions.

With the ideas of this chapter, the enquiry system proposed in the previous chapter can be enriched or widened in its analytical boundaries to account for potential contradictions and tensions occurring from creators interacting with fields and domains of knowledge. The enriched system could help creators elicit and contrast their values and conventions with those that dominate. Out of this self-awareness, creators could then venture to borrow knowledge and/ or take a stand (individually or collectively) to foster creativity in diverse ways.

With this system, creators could have the choice to align ourselves with lineages or conventions of our domains and fields of knowledge. But we could also decide not to do so, or to rethink what we see as alignment between ourselves and these elements. In the face of contradictions and the overall aim of knowledge rediscovery in society according to Abbott, creators could do 'otherwise' than expected, and that could include 'failing' in generating creative ideas. This could be the result of creators' own self-awareness about what could be the *right thing to do* in a knowledge-related situation, and also in consideration of their own ideas about *(re)connecting* themselves with their surroundings as proposed in the previous chapter of this book.

Concluding remarks

This chapter has enriched the systems model of creativity with an insight on how knowledge could unfold in society according to the sociologist Andrew Abbott. With awareness of knowledge, creators could work within new perceived constraints about how knowledge is continuously *rediscovered* within and across domains and fields. The constraint could make creators more open to exploring different avenues to validate existing knowledge, something that perhaps runs contrary to the mindsets of many of us when it comes to talking about novelty in creativity.

Considering this constraint, and with the notion of knowledge ecologies in mind, creators could then devise possibilities to think and act creatively by *borrowing* knowledge and its conventions to tackle situations. This also requires creators to be continuously aware of what is considered by convention 'the right thing to do'.

With the ideas of this chapter, the enquiry system has been enriched to help all creators identify and manage tensions or contradictions. This could be done by considering how tensions stem from creators aiming to contribute to, as well as being influenced by, relevant domains and fields of knowledge under the practice of transdisciplinary or collaborative work.

As the next chapters of this book aim to show, how creators decide to proceed in the face of knowledge dynamics would also need further reflection on doing the right thing *beyond* aligning themselves with conventions, domains and fields of knowledge.

5 Practising creativity

A self-ethnography

Introduction

The two previous chapters have provided key systems ideas to help creators understand and navigate through the complexities of their journeys. The aim was to enrich the systems model for creativity that was reviewed and presented in chapter 2. A system of enquiry was then formulated to this aim. Some of the systems ideas already presented to formulate this model have highlighted the importance of enabling self-reflection and engagement in the light of perceived tensions or dilemmas to help creators do 'the right thing'.

In the current chapter I present further reflections on using several systems ideas to pursue a creative project. This is an interpretive self-ethnographic account of my journey. There are insights, thoughts, feelings, events and possibilities which (have) help(ed) me make sense of the systemic nature of creativity as the socio-cultural school of thought for creativity proposes. In my own case and as will be shown in this chapter, a creativity project became a journey of two if not more creativities which embraced the different tensions and dilemmas experienced.

This chapter is structured as follows. The choice of methodology and structure of the chapter are laid out. Initial insights on a well-being creativity as perceived by myself are conveyed. The chapter deepens into their detail through a narrative of a 'week' in which this creativity unfolds alongside another one: pursuing a project idea. Through the chapter there are reflections in relation to the use of systems ideas for creativity. The journey concludes by going back to myself and my reflections on the journey.

Choice of method and narrative structure

For this chapter, the choice of self-ethnography as a research approach aims to unveil myself as an individual whose writing and performances constitute together a valuable source of knowledge (Denzin, 2012). The approach fits my own circumstances.

In this ethnography I perform(ed), enact(ed) and bring (brought) to life ideas which (have) constitute(d) me. I become alive and unique in the text that

I write (Ibid). The 'I' that is performed and created through the chapter is not a lone creative genius. Rather it is an 'I' who *mindfully* acknowledges his perceptions and feelings in experience, an 'I' who becomes a tool for enquiry (Wright, 2017). Because of this, the ethnography then could also help other people interpret and act upon their own perceptions and feelings (Van Maanen, 1988; Denzin, 2012).

I now speak of *creativities*, those who arise (arose) in my use of and reflection on the enquiry system previously defined and enriched to expand on and complement enquiry about the elements of Csikszentmihalyi's systems model of creativity (individuals, domains and fields of knowledge). In doing so the ethnography crafts, reveals, denounces and reflects on some cultural practices embedded in the enriched enquiry system (values, constraints, activities). These practices influence and are influenced by my pursuit of creativity. They emerge(d) in my interactions with others. The practices that are elicited – as experienced by myself – reveal the dynamics of knowledge unfolding that I came across both in managing what I call my well-being, as well as in coming up with what I regard as a creative idea for a research project.

The construction of the chapter is iterative. It is a narrated and imagined depiction of events and reflections around what constitutes one of my experienced 'days' in 'a week'. Such depiction embeds imagination, facts, feelings and thoughts, all of them being enacted as my 'reality' as a series of performative acts related to experienced events (Denzin, 2012). Along the journey of enacting, describing, interpreting and even denouncing, in the journey I pause(d) to take stock and reflect on how I use(d) the enquiring system, and how I elicit(ed) some insights that could lead me in the future to work on better understanding and acting upon issues of creativity, mental health and the use of information and communications technologies (chapter 8 of this book).

My self-ethnography can be observed as a set of specific insights and reflections, although the overall enterprise of the chapter could also be conceived of as a big reflective and systemic dialogue between individuals, creativities and the rest of our reality.

Moreover, by writing this self-ethnography, I am also showing my interpretation of inter-connected and random learning (presented in chapter 3 of this book) as an activity that will lead me to be critical about creativity (chapter 6) and to propose an encompassing, integrating and systemic ethics for creators (chapter 7).

A reunion in the 'middle of the week'

It has been more than three years since I became a user of this organisation. I ring the bell and get a warm welcome to a *self-help* group session. I used to be a regular of this group. I then had to switch to another one due to work commitments. I grab my bag to go and heat some food in the kitchen. I have made a few good friends.

No one from my official job knows I am here. I wanted to keep it this way. I still do not know if this was the right thing to do.

Despite the familiarity with this organisation, I feel strange today. I see many new faces. I know I suffered a setback a few years ago. Now, the thoughts of 'recovering' and 'moving on' from it come to my mind. For some of us, *the recovery journey is a long one*. I have been encouraged to accept this as a first and very important step. My mind tends to catastrophise situations. No one from here is asking me to leave, but I think I 'should' by now be fully recovered. 'Should' is not a good word to use.

When I first came to the self-help group, I just rang them and came along to the session – what is called *self-referral*. I was feeling anxious and somehow not able to see beyond my setback. What could have caused it this time? Could it have been moving to a new house along with looking after our newly born twins? Or was it a string of unexpected events at work combined with financial worries?

As a male, I was brought up to face up to adversity, to man up. Stress or anxiety is something that you just put up with. Quietly.

I am now more aware of my stress triggers: overdoing things (perfectionism), saying yes too much to people by fear of losing their approval (having loose boundaries) and experiencing sudden changes.

Also, the winter seasons and I are not great friends. In this group session today, I share my worry with the group: I feel great during the summer but am not sure how I will feel later in the year. Our facilitator reframes my thoughts and invites me to see that change is permanent in our lives, so why not accept it? I find it difficult to do so. Maybe that is why I study systems thinking!

Creativity as well-being

During my 'recovery' from a setback, I have made good progress in managing my perfectionist habits. I consider that I have become more *creative* about my week – in other words I have adopted a novel and valuable (at least by myself, my self-help group and my family) lifestyle. I now combine outdoor walking, painting, creative writing, mindfulness meditation, crafting, resting, watching TV, reading science fiction or history, simply going to the movies, playing golf, swimming or having a coffee with friends, some of whom have also suffered setbacks.

All of this is in the name of being more compassionate with myself, something that I have recognised as being important during group and individual mindfulness sessions and with the help of facilitators.

Also, in the last few months I have become better at saying no to commitments and feel less guilty when changing my mind. There are occasions, though, when work gets to me and I feel overwhelmed and incapable of speaking out. Too much and intensive contact with students or meetings make me drained. I want to do well, but it is physically impossible. After seeing several general practitioners and a counsellor, I was shocked to hear their verdict: *You could and would need to do something about your job*. It has taken me time to come to terms with this realisation. I love my job, perhaps too much. I need to love myself a bit more.

Because of this and because of my creativity in recovery, I now take breaks more often during the week if I can afford to. I try to listen to my body and what it is telling me. If feeling tired, I take naps on the office floor using a mat and a cushion I have there. In the last year I had to raise a concern to managers due to inevitable overwork towards the end of the working week. It took me some time to stop feeling guilty about this, but now I see it as part of looking after myself, something I did not adequately learn when growing up in my home country.

Now our human resource unit knows about me and has provided some advice and support. Nevertheless, I keep fighting my yearly workload and the culture of individualism at the place where I work. I don't know yet how things will unfold. As mentioned before, *the recovery journey is a long one*.

As I write this, I reflect on how I have used an enquiry system to help me deal with tensions when I try to be creative about what I term my personal well-being. Activities of random and inter-connected learning, borrowing and mindful experiencing have helped me to involve more of myself than just my academic and analytical brain; they also have helped me to start acknowledging serendipity and failure in my efforts both to work on my well-being and to formulate a creative project at work.

Through time, I have also acknowledged that I value being more *compassion-ate* with myself and others and not being too worried about the length of my own recovery journey. I now try to learn from my self-help group as much as possible. Also, I have met new people. Some of them have become good friends.

Through time, other enquiry ideas like beating or redesigning the system encourage me to be more proactive, talk more assertively with other people or even decide on thinking of smaller and more doable research projects in consideration of my own well-being. It helps that I feel more self-confident and assertive. At work, I try to do unto to the work systems what they do unto me (Ackoff and Rovin, 2005). For example, I delay replying to last-minute requests. I am more careful to assess my responses in the light of potential stress for myself.

I do this despite what my self-help group facilitators say: "Be careful with your energy!" Perhaps being fair and compassionate requires me to first focus on myself. But it is difficult for me to do so. I still want to do what I think is right at work and with my family. I grew up not too much accustomed to look after myself. I want to generate ideas to help myself and others.

> *I feel constrained. I am torn between the different roles or different 'selves' that I am assuming to develop my creativity (M.C. Bateson, 1994; Pope, 2005). I need to be a father, family member, academic, user, researcher. How can I manage these different selves? Should I manage?*

As the preceding diagram and the following sections show, in my enquiry I often *try and fail* to be creative with my well-being during the week. Failure has to do with not looking properly after myself, engaging too much with others

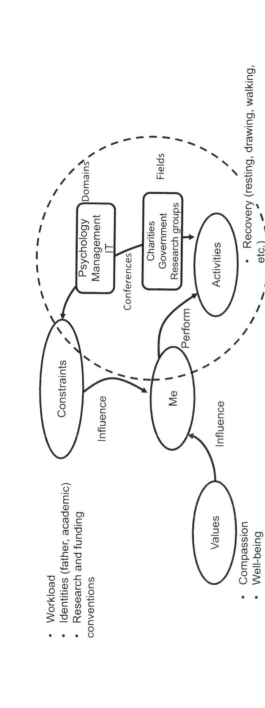

Figure 5.1 My enquiry system

and generating a good work research project idea. The latter involves interacting (often randomly) with people in several domains and fields of knowledge through conferences and other activities (including writing this book!). I refer to some of the ideas of the enquiry.

The following is a diary of my week.

The week goes by: well-being and a project

Monday

I venture in doing my creativity research and writing parts of this book or preparing teaching material. My mind is fresh. I feel motivated. I set out some goals to achieve by the end of the week. I keep a diary that registers the things I do to look after myself and the things I do about other commitments (work and family mainly).

The morning usually goes by quickly whilst I crack on with some emailing, preparing material or writing small bits of this book or research articles. Sometimes I have lunch with a colleague/friend and do some more work (usually reading) in the first part of the afternoon. I start noticing that I feel anxious because I realise that my friend/colleague has different ambitions to mine about work. I feel pulled in different directions. We go back to our office.

I usually leave work late on Mondays. On the way home, I stop at the supermarket, where I do more writing at a café inside. I encounter a mum that I know. We both have twins and used to go to a twins' club that is run by parents (mainly women). She complains about her daughters' behaviour; we talk about the club's Christmas party, and we quickly say goodbye before her twins disappear; she might go to Yoga later.

Wow, she still has energy! I know that she and I see things differently when it comes to organising childcare and family holidays. Perhaps I am still not fully adapted to the British way of managing money, jobs and children. My wife and I look after the twins on our own. There is no extended family around. When I occasionally think about this, I feel worried. However, I have learned to let go of this thought, or think about how well we have done so far.

When arriving at home in the evening, I do a bit of mindfulness meditation in the car. I also meet my neighbour with whom I have been meaning to talk about creativity (he is an artist and a musician). I take a long walk around our block to relax a bit. I get inside our house and get a warm reception from the twins, who ask me to play with them. I first eat a bit and do what I can. I feel tired but excited.

I clean the dining table, set off the dishwasher and take my anxiety medication. This is the second one I am using as the first one made me too sleepy. I get changed and watch videos with the twins on a tablet. My wife reads a book. She has looked after the twins the whole afternoon. I put them to bed. I keep watching videos, and then we both go to sleep.

Tuesday

Tuesdays have become slow-paced. My brain does not work as fast as I want it to. I wake up with some anxiety and tiredness. It did not help that one of the twins woke us up in the middle of the night. My wife and I are both irritated but in different ways. We both could do with more sleep. When I grew up I could not express my feelings of anger for fear of looking 'not well behaved' or of upsetting my parents or showing weakness. We get ready for school, drop the twins off, do a bit of shopping and I then go to work.

On arrival at the office, I feel that I need to catch up at work, and feel motivated to continue with my writing. I read and write, prepare teaching material and email a few people. I know myself a bit better now after two years. I know that tomorrow (Wednesday), I will be very tired even though I am motivated to carry on. I go to my mindfulness session, have coffee with a friend and then go to do more writing at the supermarket.

When arriving at home (sometimes later than expected) I keep the routine of helping with some household chores. I long to be my old self, adventurous, energetic and perfectionist . . . but it is proving very difficult. Especially with having two jobs (home and work).

Another Tuesday

Some of my Tuesdays I spend outside university as I have become interested in knowing a bit more about mental health and technology. I now know a friend from the Thursday self-help groups who suffers from anxiety and has not had a job for several years. Every other Tuesday she goes to the job centre. I have been with her several times, and she introduces me to the job advisor (now career coach) as a friend who gives moral support.

Due to her anxiety (and I learned bits more about family upbringing and having been bullied at school in our self-help group) my friend would often 'misread' what the career coach would say to her. In the first two minutes of the meeting my friend becomes very anxious and bordering on the aggressive. The meetings could turn into some misfiring of messages. My friend would recite her account of what she has been doing since the last meeting. This includes receiving training, phoning companies, visiting them, sharpening up her CV, sending it to companies or preparing covering letters with the help of an advocate from our charitable organisation, etc.

The three of us know that my friend is anxious to get her employment seeking allowance approved for the next two weeks. My friend has come to call it 'my money'. Between conversations, the allowance gets approved, and my friend gets more relaxed.

The coach tries her best not to upset my friend and gives my friend advice, material or leaflets. On one occasion, the coach and I had to push my friend to acknowledge that she needed to overcome her fear of computers. In different ways we raised the importance of tuning in with how applying for jobs works nowadays.

Partly thanks to the help she received in our group, my friend now knows where she wants to work. It took her a long time to realise this. She is doing some related volunteering and is enjoying it. She still finds it difficult, though, to search for jobs online. Fortunately, she gets some support from us and other charity organisations. The support depends, though, on kind individuals willing to help her.

Reflection

My interpretation of these meetings leads me to connect two separate 'contexts' or 'worlds': one of mental health, another of job seeking. The meeting enables these two worlds to con-nect, albeit briefly. These worlds seem to have different goals: to improve well-being and to put people in jobs. Perhaps this set of contradictory goals is what gives rise to tensions and anxieties for my friend.

As the preceding figure shows, in both worlds there are also unresolved issues with technology. People in these worlds have some degree of control over technology, but they still must live with sudden changes or the lack of support when it comes to mastering it. There is some support that in my view could be much improved.

After the meeting at the job centre we go for a coffee with my friend. I real-ise she has a point when it comes to using computers or technology. I also think

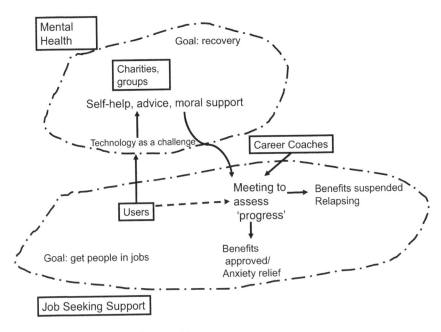

Figure 5.2 An encounter of two worlds

that she could be less anxious in the first few minutes of the meeting. Easier said than done. But I also know from my own experience that when my stress and worries take over I cannot think straight or focus well.

So now I am thinking of a creative idea for a research project: *to improve support for people like my friend who are dealing with employability issues and are using technology.*

This is something I could enjoy. I am still not sure if I am internally or externally motivated to pursue this creative idea (Csikszentmihalyi, 1988; Amabile, 1998). *What is driving me: Is it my interest to help others, to connect with different people, to be recognised at work?*

After having coffee with my friend, I drive home. There is heavy traffic, and I arrive completely exhausted. I do not talk much to my children or play. I think I overstretched my available energy today. I feel stressed and anxious because I am thinking I am not a good father.

Who do I want to be? What sort of work-life balance do I want to have? This last question was asked by a counsellor when I had my setback. I still do not have a clear answer to it.

Also, my group facilitator friend has warned me several times that I really need time to myself. Any idea for a project or any help to anyone else must consider first what she calls my well-being.

Wednesday

In the morning I argue with my wife. I say to her that I am not a perfect human being: I feel tired and not able to do what she asks for. The week has been overwhelming so far, and I feel tired and drained. I finally share some of my feelings with her. I feel worried and stressed. We both need to relax. I need to regain control over myself.

On the way to work, I stop and take a walk in a park. I feel a bit more relaxed. For some reason I think that life has become too complex. I hope I can become less worried and anxious. I am like one of my grandparents.

Now that I feel more relaxed, the idea for a project comes back to my mind. I try to focus on enjoying my walk. I get back to my car and do some mindfulness. I also nap for a little while.

At work I meet colleagues to talk about another similar potential project. Over several coffee meetings on Wednesdays with them, we find some interesting commonalities. I decide to share my initial project idea with them.

Two reflections

In potentially pursuing this idea with colleagues in an interdisciplinary research project (something we have been asked to do by our university), I also think that here could be opportunities for 'borrowing' ideas or methods of analysis from different disciplines (Abbot, 2004): management, psychology, information systems or computer science. We have talked about doing systematic literature reviews (popular in psychology), scanning of eye movements (also popular in human computer interaction) and participative evaluation of computer use (also popular in applied systems thinking). For my psychology colleague, participation comes mostly when designing any research study, whereas for myself it could be continuous.

As academics, these colleagues and I belong to different 'lineages' (psychology, management, human computer interaction, systems thinking). We would like to have a project. We want to use some of our previous expertise and existing knowledge. As a kind of implicit convention, we want to be resourceful and 'kill two or more birds with one stone'.

My own take on the project changes through time. A snapshot of my heuristic borrowing strategies is shown in the following table. When iterating through them, I become aware that both knowledge and funding conventions dictate what the right thing to do is, so that borrowing of ideas or methods would need to be filtered out in the light of what people in various domains (psychology, computer science) and fields (government and funding agencies mainly) consider 'novel' and 'doable' if not 'impactful'.

From the possibilities that arise when using borrowing strategies, it could well be that the problems derived from mental health services users utilising technology to improve their employability opportunities are politically motivated as well as structurally endemic in society. If this is the case, any idea for a project will have to consider how employment and the use of technology are wider societal phenomena. Addressing them would also require thinking about the purpose of a project and, with it, the purpose of creativity.

Borrowing helps me to freely venture to think of several possibilities and discuss them with collaborators. These possibilities could also help me refine

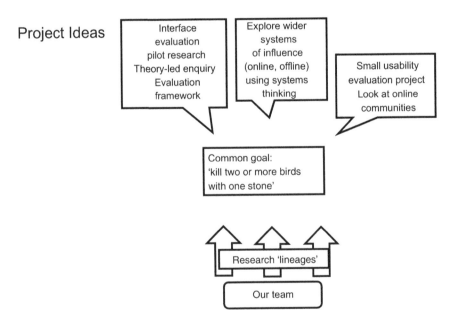

Figure 5.3 Creativity at work

my own thinking and acting as a creator. I could venture to share them with my collaborators. To do so, I need to overcome my own fear of changing my mind. I know I have the right to do so, but still this feels like an obstacle to overcome in my creativity at work.

I also become more aware of cognitive and 'political' aspects of my creativities alongside my own experience of them. *I am still unsure about the best way to pursue the project idea further. Doing so for me will involve more work, and, if successful, managing a project. I keep asking myself about my motivation to do it. I need to be creative about how I can handle a project on top of my existing workload. Maybe a smaller project or having a PhD student to work on it? I would not like to feel that I am putting myself at risk of having another setback due to stress or overwork. I also wonder: Will I be able to take this idea/project opportunity to learn about myself and them as Abbott suggests rather than simply embarking to 'rediscover' knowledge rather than advance it?*

Also, by practising mindfulness meditation and doing some things that I like outside work, I am becoming more mindful about my project, which also involves my own well-being. I have been creative about myself, and by doing that I have become engaged in pursuing a creative idea. I see myself as both an individual and a collaborator when it comes to defining whom I am as a creator. I have also inter-connected with different individuals within and beyond work. It has helped that I can also see myself as merely a user of the organisation mentioned earlier in this chapter.

Table 5.1 Heuristic borrowing for a project idea

Type of heuristics	Description	Strategies for iteration
Search heuristic	Looking outside an area	❖ Analogies: Is the use of IT by expert users a political problem of access or a managerial/technical problem of support?
Fractal heuristic	Looking at debates in social science	➢ Is this a problem of choice (willing to be IT literate) versus constraint (not enough support resources)?
		➢ Is this a problem of conflict (between capitalism and socialism) or consensus (dialogue and participation can help provide resources to address it)?
		➢ Is this a problem of transcendent (generic) vs situated knowledge on IT support/access?
		➢ Or is this a problem of agency (user's IT literacy) versus structure (endemic social marginalisation)?
Argument heuristic	Looking within a phenomenon: Is this 'really' true?	▪ Is lack of IT support causing mental health problems, or are mental health problems causing lack of IT support?
		▪ Is this really a persistent problem? How far can we go if we do not treat it as such?

The rest of my Wednesday I reduce my workload but still carry on. I take more coffee to get some energy to do a bit more writing or attending work meetings (I get worked up in these meetings; not sure yet how to best cope with them).

After meetings (or when I feel tired), I take a nap in my office for about half an hour. Then I get ready for the next day and leave work. Back home, I help a bit. My mind has lots of ideas and worries about work.

Before going to bed I feel anxious. There are warnings about my mood. I was supposed to rest a bit more today after two busy days. However, given the excitement and my desire to regain control over my work, I did not pay attention to what my body was telling me.

How can I get back to looking after my well-being? Is that something that I have been brought up to do only during weekends? How can I be creative about stopping mid-week?

Thursday

I leave the house tired and in two minds. Not sure about attending an event at work or a conference outside it, I go for the latter.

This *conference* on mental health provides me with good insights and contact possibilities for the project I am now pursuing. There are many interesting presentations. Some of them are more scientific or managerial than others. Some users of mental health services (experts by experience) also give their testimonies. There is poetry, and drama performances, which I find very touching.

I hear about other conditions like autism and the importance of socialisation or getting the right kind of support according to one's condition. I learn about change as something that is not particularly easy to achieve given our brain configurations and history. I keep taking notes during the presentations and after talking to people over coffee.

In the conference, there is a variety of organisations providing services, including the one whose self-help groups I attend. Some organisations are bigger than others, and their language and means of communication appear to me a bit conventional. Others seem to be more open to new ideas or possibilities, and their language also speaks more with other aids like videos rather than leaflets. Other organisations seem to lean more towards enabling co-ordinated action or pointing people to other organisations and their services.

After attending some of the talks I now feel tired. Maybe it is because this is a new environment for me, and I spent a great deal trying to learn new things.

A reflection

Yes, by following my curiosity I have ventured to explore a kind of random situation with the view to combine what I know about mental health with learning something new – to play a dual role (academic and user by experience). As mentioned in chapter 3 of this book, I am now more aware of the importance of also learning coping strategies with consideration of my own mind-body circumstances (M.C. Bateson, 2006). I see now more clearly that creativity is not only about pursuing creative ideas but also learning to adapt, and taking one step at a time.

For me, a key issue in pursuing this learning is to ask for help and listen to my body. I think that there are also cultural factors which inhibit us from talking openly about ourselves. Myself, I was brought up to not let my guard down. Maybe this puts additional strain on my mood and my energy.

I know that unless I have time for myself, I will not have a good rest of the week. Given my perfectionist habits, I am now berating myself for not looking after myself and for overdoing things. I get home and do my bit of domestic chores.

Fortunately, I have a great wife. I do not know what I would do without her.

Interestingly a speaker suggests we need to learn more about the cultural background of people with mental health conditions. This speaker says that many of us just need someone to talk to, as we feel alienated from a society that has different norms and values. Perhaps my setback had also to do with me moving to a new area and finding it difficult to integrate into or feel part of it.

I get to talk to different people both as an academic and as an experienced user. I get to hear more from a benefits advisor about the new approach by job centres of having career coaches. Nowadays they seem to be more flexible and less punitive when helping people who have mental disabilities. They adopt a more therapeutic approach. Progress in this approach is not about reporting job seeking, but about working holistically with the individual. Here is me again thinking in terms of systems.

I also get to talk to a civil servant who kindly offers some ideas about advocacy. She has first-hand experience in her family of mental health issues as well as job centres. She, the benefits advisor and a very friendly counsellor (both of whom speak my own native language) give me their contact details.

A reflection

I have gained interesting insights about mental health and how it involves connections between different groups and organisations. They all have different interests and ways of conceiving of creativity. As an ecology or series of knowledge ecologies (Abbott, 2005), mental health includes diverse organisations and groups. There are also poets, actors and entrepreneurs who previously have also been expert users. Some have set up their own initiatives in the form of social enterprises. Other entrepreneurs come from 'outside' the mental health ecology and are currently developing technology solutions.

My own interpretation of creativity in this sort of knowledge ecology of mental health involving myself, my collaborators and other groups can be depicted in the following systems model.

As the figure shows, there are creative persons as groups of entrepreneurs, (health) professionals and users by experience, all of them aiming to generate valuable ideas and projects (e.g. social enterprises, technology apps). These individuals become loosely connected through some general activities (e.g. conferences).

Creators like myself are supported by groups (e.g. self-help, well-being, family). These groups do not seem to feature in Csikszentmihalyi's (1988) original systems model of

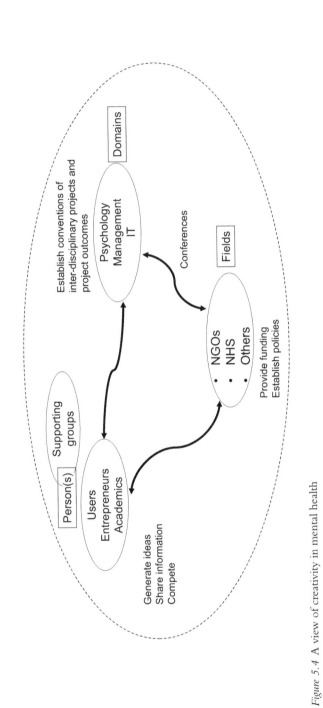

Figure 5.4 A view of creativity in mental health

creativity. They might not be bounded by the dynamics of integration and differentiation that he and collaborators suggest (Csikszentmihalyi and Wolfe, 2000; Routledge et al., 2008). For me, though, these groups have helped greatly in my journey of recovery and in shaping my creative ideas about my well-being and a project. They have also opened my mind to interact with others on the topic of mental health.

In the figure, government and other organisations act as gatekeepers of fields of knowledge. They provide spaces for people to meet and exchange ideas. They also provide funding opportunities and formulate relevant policies. Creativity emerges from the interaction of these elements in two forms:

1   Dealing with day-to-day situations for both users and supporters. The latter's creativity can be regarded in terms of using resources wisely, sharing information and coming up with ideas.
2   For expert users, creativity means recovering, staying well or venturing to formulate a new initiative to help themselves or others.

As I infer from the figure, the connection between individual creators and domains is a weak one. Management academics like myself could be interested in mental health, and more could be done to strengthen links with mental health users, health professionals and entrepreneurs. We could learn a bit more from other domains like psychology or computer science as I have been doing. Sustaining this type of learning, however, requires energy.

Towards the end of this conference, the master of ceremonies (someone whom everybody knows) recaps some key messages to take home which to me bear importance to creativity in this ecology of mental health:

- Don't forget about art! It is therapeutic.
- Human beings are capable of the most wonderful empathetic acts.
- There are challenges, not problems.
- Our biggest fear is to discover how powerful we are or can become.
- There is a succession of generations working together now.

The conference was a challenge to step out of my comfort zone and venture to learn new things about mental health. I learned lots more but at the price of stretching my energy.

I now lack energy. I take the bus to go home, knowing that I am tired. I need to wind down and look after myself. I could feel that I, in my mind and body, was experiencing flow at this event (the time went by very quickly, I was coming up with lots of interesting ideas, I felt I had good connections with some people there). I was not able to stop and look after myself properly, though.

Friday

At the self-help group (this one is for well-being) we talk about how our week has been (it is called checking-in); we listen and give support or advice. Then we engage in crafty activities like drawing, colouring, planting, pottery, etc. To me it feels like I am developing aspects of myself that I had forgotten. This is part of my well-being creativity.

It is *creativity back again*, individually tailored, little 'c', well-being related. A project to work on myself. *The journey is a long one.*

I feel surrounded by brave and experienced individuals who often deal on their own with lots of things that life throws at them. I feel listened to and valued. I can laugh or cry. I can speak or remain silent. It is a safe space to be myself.

Today, the last day of the working week, I openly share that I am tired and feel guilty about not taking time to myself. I get encouraging feedback about taking the rest of the day off or doing something that takes my mind off worries and helps me wind down. I also get a different view about work. I do what I can, that is all.

Somebody asks: "How much difference will it make to continue putting effort into doing something before 'letting it go' [i.e. a research paper or a project idea] and *accepting whatever comes afterwards* [success or failure]?"

My brother Ricardo would say: "A rabbit can continue biting the same carrot without considering if there are better carrots elsewhere".

Wise words . . .

I go to my office and take a long nap after lunch. I also watch 'trash TV'. These things lift my energy levels. I get home in a calmer mood.

The weekend

My mind thinks I am physically younger. Not being mindful of my lack of energy, I overdo the father role. On Saturday, after taking the twins out (fathers club first Saturday of each month, or recycling items), and doing some cooking, I become irritable.

I did not read the signs of my body. My perfectionist habits are ingrained.

I cry. I tell my family I need a rest. I force myself to lie down. I feel guilty.

This has happened again. *I cannot say much.* I am angry with myself.

The mood in my house changes. I manage to help somehow with bathing the twins and putting them to bed. I immerse myself watching TV on my tablet. *I cannot say much.*

On Sunday, I feel embarrassed. I could not look after myself properly during the week, and as a result I ended up affecting my family.

We go about business as usual: Going to Church or me staying home decorating, taking the twins to a park, cooking something quickly or possibly going to a children's birthday party.

I cannot say much.

I am now punishing myself, berating myself. I ask my wife to forgive my outbursts. We bathe the twins, and watch some videos (all of us on different tablets). I put the twins to bed, we keep watching TV on our tablets and we get to sleep. I now know that I will wake up feeling energetic, my 'old self', able to deal with lots of things, even if that is for a couple of days before realising I cannot be this old self anymore.

Another week gone.

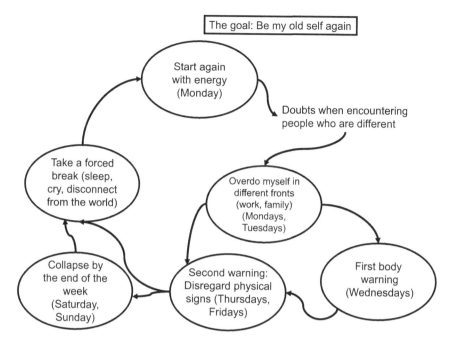

Figure 5.5 A week of creativity

Afterword

I have tried to break the cycle described in this chapter, with some success. I am now more aware of when I feel tired and have begun to explore ways of resting mid-week. I am more careful with my workload and my energy at home.

Over the next few months I will be visiting government and non-government organisations to get feedback on my project idea. I will be discussing the idea further with colleagues, competitors and potential funders in meetings and conferences.

There is a good interest. Between colleagues there are differences, though. Some want to look at ergonomic or psychological factors that affect the use of technology by people. Myself, I want to help broadening technological and non-technological support.

Feedback received from many potential project stakeholders or collaborators is encouraging, as they find the idea appealing. They want to frame it, though, in terms of what they think is going to get funding and is going to 'work' for them. I need to know more about their knowledge conventions, what they consider relevant and how they think research is to be done. Their notions of research are different from mine.

In venturing to randomly explore and learn from other contexts as the Batesons suggest (chapter 3), I can see some environmental if not cultural *differences*.

Government stakeholders will ask lots of questions, whereas other stakeholders will give support if the project is aligned to their values and mission. There are hierarchies and territories in academia and beyond that I need to know more about. There are also differences between what they and I mean by mental health.

> *Will I be able to let go and do the right thing for me? Or will I continue trying to accommodate other people's demands, to be a perfectionist people pleaser?*

In the last year and due to external circumstances, my teaching workload has increased considerably. I have not been able to regularly attend my self-help groups nor to carry on with mindful meditation as much as I used to. I am partly to blame for this. I now know that I need to continue saying no and raising my own concerns to systems at work. I also need to have time and space to do things that revitalise me.

For the enquiry system to support creators like me, with regards to the experiences described in this chapter, for creators there need to be *activities of self-care, guided by a value with the same name and constrained by our own biological condition that requires us to manage our energy.*

A final reflection

So much for me trying to become my old self again. For my creative project ideas and for aiming to do the right thing in whatever aspect of my life, I need to get back to my own well-being. For the time being, I must learn to really stop earlier during the week, to invest more time in myself and to say no to my enthusiasm.
The recovery journey is a long one.

Concluding remarks

This chapter has provided a self-ethnographic account of my own journey into creativity using the enquiry system as a reflective tool. I have been able to distinguish creativities related to what I consider my own well-being and a project to make the best of personal circumstances.

My journey started with my own well-being and how being creative about it has helped me. A first type of creativity was then identified. In this type of creativity, the use of systems ideas focused on mindful experiencing and giving myself opportunities to be compassionate and less judgemental with myself.

Dealing with these two creativities was a main generator of tensions and contradictions. As my well-being recovery progressed, I also became more mindful of the need to manage it with my pursuit of a creative project. Activities of mindful experiencing in the form of mindful meditation and self-help groups, randomly learning and becoming more aware of my own research conventions, lineage and reactions to existing systems at work have helped me to identify the importance of self-care. Further pursuing creativity at work requires, however, to get back to my own well-being creativity, and use it as an anchor as the following diagram suggests.

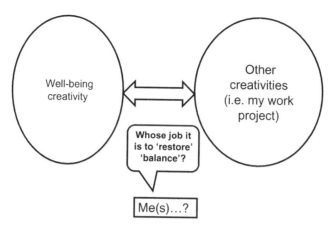

Figure 5.6 Restoring 'balance' between creativities

Reflecting on such identification for myself as a creator also becomes important to be critical about this ideal of achieving balance. I need to further reflect on why/if/how myself, a creative individual, like a lone genius, is to be made *(solely) responsible* for keeping or restoring balances between my creativities.

How is it possible that such a balance has become
essential in the life of someone like me?

My own critique of the systems model in relation to dealing with contradictions in the face of complexity can also apply to the enriched enquiry system and its assumptions. In both cases, contradictions are acknowledged, *but only up to a point*. The responsibility of reconciling them (now restoring a balance between creativities) is left to creators. That could become more difficult if creators decide not to be one with their creativities, or critically analyse the assumption that, as creators, we all have an opportunity to connect to the universe to fulfil (Csikszentmihalyi, 1998).

There is the possibility of exerting critical caution about the use of systems thinking itself as is being initially suggested by applied systems thinking (see chapter 3). This would mean revisiting some of the taken-for-granted assumptions and being critical about them. Systems thinking ideas for managing creativity would need to challenge *if and how* existing ethical values, cultures and ways of doing things in organisations and societies (including the use of systems models) could contribute to limiting the potential of individuals.

In this regard, we would need to better understand how systems thinking and creativity, and more specifically the use of the enquiry system to deal with contradictions and tensions, have become somehow *accepting* of the conventions and divides of knowledge, the separation between creativity and ethics and the effects having to deal almost individually with serendipity, 'shit', success or failure. A systemic view of creativity needs to be also systemic about the effects of creativity.

To address this, in the next chapter of this book, creativity is studied from the perspective of governmentality. I leave the reader with some thoughts that I have identified during mindful experiences during my creative journeys and which I hope could be of some help.

- I want to be my old self: brainy, career oriented, ambitious.
- I am not good enough.
- I fear failure.
- I fear the disapproval of others.
- I think it is my fault.
- I value too much analysing and solving problems.
- I am different, idealistic and sensitive.
- I am analytical, introverted, perceptual, and I can be led by feelings about myself and others.
- I am not my job, my writing or my reputation.
- I have a great and loving family.
- I do not need to be perfect; doing OK will do.
- I am learning to quit earlier than what I normally expect.
- I am a human being. I can change my mind. I can have bad days.
- I would like to live a simple life, live in a small town, have time for my writing and socialise.
- Maybe there is no balance, or a next big level to achieve in life!

6   Governing creativity

Introduction

The previous chapter has shown how exciting, whilst complex and profound, creativity can be when we as creators use systems ideas to study, advance or reflect on it.

For myself, developing a creative project whilst recovering from a setback entailed a journey involving my own well-being and some relevant knowledge ecologies in the pursuit of a creative project. Creativity situations involved being resourceful and dealing with work-life balance tensions or contradictions, one of them being the need to slow down in my efforts whilst advancing (self) knowledge. During this journey, diverse ideas, goals and perspectives emerged. I found that I needed to continuously pay attention to what I wanted to get out of my project idea as well as to whom I wanted to become as a human being.

Creativity – or in my case creativities – became influenced by implicit rules about what counted as creative knowledge, as well as about how creators could be 'allowed' to operate as such (i.e. by working in transdisciplinary and potentially impactful efforts). This also included the very same idea of well-being, and how it required me to learn to regulate if not balance my 'self'.

I could somehow and 'freely' engage with ideas, projects or activities. But given my own character as a somewhat 'perfectionist', 'hands-on' and 'can-do' person, my creativity journey became longer and more complex and stressful than initially expected.

I could now perceive the systemic nature of creativity and its features ('shit', serendipity, failure) when it also came to think of myself as a creator. My project idea emerged somehow in an unintended way from my random well-being interactions. These interactions have also led me to consider how much I am willing to stretch myself at work and what I regard as 'success': at work, I need to beat existing notions if I am to continue recovering from a setback.

I have also become critical of the idea that doing the right thing is linked to my creativities.

From the self-ethnography presented in the previous chapter of this book, it can be posited that the use of systems ideas for creativity needs further reflection. There is an issue that deserves to be revisited and explored further, and which I have also written about previously (Córdoba-Pachón, 2010): how dealing with attempts to improve situations becomes a reflection of *whom we want to become as subjects in the light of power relations, those that shape how we think and act and those we could influence.* In this way, creativity and ethics, my desire to do the right things and striving to live a 'good' life become connected in the face of power.

To further explore this connection between creativity and ethics, and with a view to enhancing critical thinking about creativity and its 'balanced' management, the current chapter considers how creativities and those subjects involved or affected by them could be *governed.* Michel Foucault's ideas on governmentality and some of its extensions are presented and used. The aim is to advance the argument that awareness of creativity as a governing set of incomplete enterprises could help creators become 'someone else', whilst still aiming to be creative in different ways of thinking and acting.

By identifying and analysing forms of *governing* that surround our creativities, creators could then be better prepared to work on ourselves as ethical subjects who – in the face of power relations – might pursue, rework or even let go of our ideas about ourselves (i.e. identities) and others. This could then help us redefine the boundaries of enquiry systems like the one that has been proposed and used in this book.

This chapter is organised as follows. The possibility to complement systems ideas with a self-critique of 'whom we have become' as creators is raised. Michel Foucault's ideas on governmentality are presented, and some elements of critical analysis are drawn from them. Then, an analysis of how both well-being and creativity have contributed to shape whom I have become is initially proposed. Some possibilities to use these forms for what I think could be my benefit and that of others are elicited.

Creativity as governing

As a creator, and following from my self-ethnographic reflections, I still want to see how my creativities came about, and what I can do to reunite if not challenge them. I would also like to enable others to do the same. The self-ethnography revealed that in practice, I was 'nudged' to be more creative to explore better ways to know and manage myself as an individual and family member, something that nowadays governments are prone to support (Thaler, 2009). At work, I became aware of the dynamics that unfolded when attempting to create a project idea by interacting with others and borrowing knowledge: I had somehow to 'frame' an idea according to certain rules or conventions that influenced what counted as 'creative' within knowledge ecologies. Creativity thus required inter-disciplinary knowledge collaboration, which in turn was being promoted by organisational policies in academic settings and beyond. Persevering in pursuing an idea also required adopting procedures and ways of working that could see an idea being 'agreed', 'approved' if not 'funded'.

Moreover, in my interactions with others I needed to be open to learning whilst co-operative when formulating research projects; use language that others could understand; use existing funding schemes; and make sure that the project (if funded) would then generate research impact. My creativity needed to follow these indirect and influential ways of thinking/acting to be accepted as successful.

This also included my thinking and acting as an individual seeking to improve his well-being. I somehow became more reflective on my own 'recovery progress' and could also show this progress to others via periodical conversational or written self-assessments; these seem to be part of conventions used to generate and disseminate knowledge across government and non-government organisations, and to support further requests for funding. As I write this, the organisation that I am a user of is nudging both facilitators and users to be more 'structured' in our activities, so that the organisation can demonstrate to their funders 'value for donations'. This seems to have become a common practice now in the UK third and public sectors.

For the French scholar Michel Foucault, modern ideas about knowledge, modern society and the 'free' human subject can be considered historically contingent. They have emerged in circumstances which deserve to be analysed, so that people can better discern what needs to be kept, left or redefined. In adopting a view based on historical contingency, Foucault also encourages us to become aware of the dangers that any idea (i.e. 'creativity', 'creator') could pose for our present and our future. Even if as individuals we decide to live like 'hermits' or 'heroes', this would have implications for how we decide to conduct ourselves.

The interest in the individual 'I' as a subject in the nineteenth century Western world was to Foucault a manifestation of the operation of power *relations* between people and influenced how we would see ourselves as perishable, and hence in need of managing as well as being managed in our biological existence (Foucault 1979, 1990 and 2009). In several areas of life, being (self-)managed would be influenced by ideas and practices about what counted as human life and how it needed to be managed. Relevant decisions would be made in parallel to the establishment of what knowledge was to be considered relevant and who or what aspect of being human was to become a subject of interest.

According to Foucault (Ibid), forms of power over the human body and its existence (bio-power) had a previous 'incarnation', so to speak. There was a possibly broader manifestation of Christianity-based pastoral power. Such relations unfolded in the rise of Christianity and modern states in Western Europe. They resulted in forms of subordination, obedience and self-control. Given its Christian roots, pastoral power entailed also the renunciation of a role in this world, and, through self-discipline and self-examination of one's consciousness, something that also had some manifestations in classic Greek and Roman societies.

During the nineteenth century and with the delimitation of territorial boundaries between states, the human populations inhabiting them became in need to be accounted for and administered (Foucault, 1978 and 1979). The notion of *population* became relevant to allow for it to be managed in similar ways to existing family households. To account for knowledge distinctions and practices associated with the management of populations and citizens, Foucault (1978) thus proposed an analytical element to facilitate critical thinking about government-oriented power.

This element was called by Foucault 'governmentality'. It was to inherit some features of pastoral power, now operating at both individual and collective levels and pervading different domains of life.

Governmentality, conduct and freedom

In basic terms, governmentality involves the managing of people, things and relations between these (Foucault, 1978). There are different power elements involving explicit discourses and norms, ways of seeing and acting, authorities and established forms of compliance to norms (technologies) (Rose et al., 2006). Foucault's detailed definition of governmentality in 1978 is:

1   "The ensemble formed by the institutions, procedures, analyses and reflections, the calculations and tactics that allow the exercise of this very specific albeit complex form of power, which has as its target population, as its principal form of knowledge political economy, and as its essential technical means apparatuses of security.

2   The tendency which, over a long period and throughout the West, has steadily led towards the pre-eminence over all other forms (sovereignty, discipline, etc.) of this type of power which may be termed government, resulting, on the one hand, in the formation of a whole series of specific governmental apparatuses, and, on the other, in the development of a whole complex of *savoirs*.

3   The process, or rather the result of the process, through which the state of justice in the Middle Ages, transformed into the administrative state during the fifteenth and sixteenth centuries, gradually becomes 'governmentalised'" (Foucault, 1978, pp. 102–103).

According to Foucault (1978, 1979 and 2009), modern states could strengthen their positions both politically and militarily through governmentalities that were embedded in the social body. State organisations were being made legitimate and necessary by using existing social relations of power. They did not impose themselves autocratically over their populations. Instead they could use existing social relations to structure the *conduct* of so-called free individuals and populations so that they followed established or desirable paths of thinking and action. In this regard Foucault says:

> [Government] power is exercised only over *free* subjects, and only insofar as they are free. By this we mean individual or collective subjects who are faced with a field of possibilities in which several ways of behaving, several reactions and diverse comportments, may be realized.
>
> (Foucault, 1982a, pp. 789–790, italics and brackets added)

The diversity of possibilities for the manifestation of governmentalities also reveals how in a situation under analysis, there could be different ways in which individuals might think they are freely exercising their will when in fact they are being organised, directed or structured (Foucault, 1991). For creators this means that even if we think that we are 'running the show' in our interactions with others and driven by what we think are meaningful ideas, we could have been influenced to think, act and be in certain ways which we could identify and reflect upon (Wright, 2017).

For the field and practice of creativity, these ideas could help creators build a new layer of critique that focuses on how we and others have become whom we currently are as 'human beings' who need to be 'managed' (even with our creativity research); how governmentalities encourage us to act 'freely' and thus assume 'free' responsibility towards our efforts; and how with these efforts we fulfil societal needs to manage ourselves or be managed.

This could also mean that there could be 'other' relations that contribute to giving meaning to creativity in its different manifestations. As with the self-ethnography reported previously in this book, such relations (e.g. striking a balance or bidding for project grants) might be taken for granted when creators use systems ideas or models. There could be embedded as well influencing ingrained ways of thinking and acting in our societies.

Perhaps the reader might think that under this perspective of government power, creators are coerced by 'invisible forces' or 'hands' against which we have little or no power. However, it is important to remember that from the perspective of governmentality and considering that power operates only on 'free' subjects, the enterprise of governing is an incomplete one (Gordon, 1980; Rose et al., 2006). It is worth highlighting what Rose et al. (2006, pp. 99–101, italics added) say about creativity within government power. It can take place only within certain boundaries:

> [Government power] is not assumed to be a by-product or necessary effect of immanent social or economic forces or structures. Rather, it is an attempt by those confronting certain social conditions to make sense of their environment, to imagine ways of improving the state of affairs, and to devise ways of achieving these ends. *Human powers of creativity are centred rather than marginalized*, even though such creation takes place within certain styles of thought and must perforce make use of available resources, techniques, and so on.

Governmentality invites creators to use the freedom that is at our disposal to analyse, think and act in ways that might even run contrary to what is expected of us (Foucault, 1984a and 2009). The scope of our creativities has a dual component of predictability: Creators can engage in studying what is possible to do according to power relations; the outcome(s) of their actions cannot be fully ascertained, nor planned or managed.

Moreover, for creators it becomes important to assume that these systems are never in the individual's control, no matter how brilliant the person's work

(Hanson, 2013). With this, creators can thus have a new and valuable angle on creativity: Even if we think we can succeed by accepting it or even trying to manage it, that effort is futile in similar ways to the effort to seek to secure the 'I' within experience as discussed earlier. The best we could do is possibly to let go of the idea that we are free to act upon ourselves or others.

If as creators we are to live in society, we need to strike a deal with creativity: In the midst of societal dynamics, we can intend to use what we are given to our own advantage and within what we see as 'normal' limits for society. These limits, though, are to be maintained or regulated. As 'free' creators, our responsibility lies in striving to ensure that these limits do not erode what we can do within them – in other words that relations do not erode freedom. The striving is to be continuous, in what Foucault (1982a) calls *agonistic*, if not inciting or seductive, chess-game like power relations.

The remaining and other features of creativity including 'shit', 'serendipity', 'failure' or 'responsibility' could be left to others, in what they seek to regulate over themselves and others.

Analytical elements of governmentality

> This encounter between technologies of domination of others and those of the self I call 'governmentality'.
>
> – Foucault (1988, translated from Spanish)

Foucault's governmentality thinking has been taken forward by many researchers who were encouraged to pursue their own projects (Noguera, 2009). As a result, many of them engaged with neoliberalism and its manifestations in different realms of life (Gordon, 1991). From community relations to insurance or risk, Foucault's followers intended to reveal the possibilities and dangers of the structuring of individual and collective freedom under the emergent influence of neoliberalism (Ibid).

After his studies on governmentality, Foucault's writings became focused on critically exploring the emergence of ethics as an area of knowledge, thinking and acting (Foucault, 1994a, b; Rose et al., 2006). Foucault seems to have become less interested in exploring the formation of knowledges (*savoirs*) to govern than in identifying and promoting ideas and forms to counteract inherited, contingent and deemed unnecessary forms of conduct (Foucault, 2009). In his studies of sexuality, he provided his analyses to invite other people to review and recreate their relationships to themselves and to others.

The paths that Foucault traced could be useful for creators to develop our own ways to explore how we have become subjects of different creativities (Noguera, 2009); to tease out our particularities, visibilities and invisibilities within the social body we are part of; to find and transgress limits that have been superimposed upon us in the ways we are used to know, think or behave; and to make ourselves works of art who are in continuous reinvention (Foucault, 1984a, 1994a).

To analyse government power relations and how they shape whilst being shaped by creativity, it is also important to remember that in Foucault's work, power relations are capillary (Foucault, 1990). They operate in matrix-like forms across institutions and individual or collective levels of influence. In their operation, people can exert influence *over themselves as well as others*. Within existing power relations, we have opportunities to govern ourselves and others according to what we think needs to happen.

Furthermore, central to the analysis of power relations is the idea that they embed and are embedded in what Foucault calls 'regimes of truth' (Foucault, 1991; Gordon, 1980 and 1991). For creators this means analysis of their links: Creators/creativities like the ones identified in the previous chapter embrace ideas of what is true about them or about their creative work. There could be different ideas or notions of what it is they need to achieve for themselves and others with their creativity. Analysis would then aim to identify and explore such links, discern what is necessary and what is contingent and rework if not redefine them.

For the creativity field and to manage creativity, these insights could be used to critically analyse:

- How socio-cultural and systems thinking approaches to creativity come to operate and shape creators' discourses, practices, ways of thinking and acting; in other words, creators' *conducts*.
- What we could do within limits identified to conduct to *transgress or counterconduct* them (Foucault, 2009) for the benefit of ourselves and others.

Critically informed ethics for creativity

Foucault (1991, 1992); Gordon (1980, 1991); and Dean (2010) have proposed ways to dissect and integrate different types of power relations that impinge on, as well as could be influenced by, our *conduct* as human beings. They provide grids for the perception of reality which include what we think (we could do) about ourselves. Such relations could often be manifested in explicit discourses, as well as invisible ways of operation, which could be revealed by studying their post-hoc or non-documented effects (Kendall and Wickham, 1999).

These typologies of government power suggest its influence in collective and individual manifestations of phenomena. Following Kendall and Wickham (1999), it can be said that some power relations are explicit in discourse and practice, whereas others become visible only after their effects can be discerned. They also operate at different levels (macro, micro), constituting an apparatus of *convergences* that travels across organisations, and define human subjects as subjects of conduct via power relations.

For the field of creativity, Hanson (2013) analyses how discourses and practices on creativity contribute to fulfilling societal functions whilst making creators 'disappear'. He then suggests analysing power relations to identify limitations and opportunities that creators could build on to 'recreate themselves' continuously as works of art (Foucault, 1984a) and which entail working on

Table 6.1 Typologies of government power

Author	Foucault (1992, pp. 25–30)	Gordon (1980, 1991)	Dean (2010, inspired by Foucault, 1992)
Level of analysis	Individual	Individual/collective	Individual/collective
Description	Determination of the *ethical substance* or ways in which the individual constitutes part of oneself as prime material of ethical conduct; *mode of subjection* or the way to establish a relation to a norm; *forms of elaboration*, techniques or ways to perform on oneself to bring compliance to the norm; and *telos*, a certain mode of being that is pursued via transformation of oneself	**Programmes**: declared and explicit discourses that define a reality of subjects that needs to be governed, together with the knowledge and socially embedded practices to meet goals that are never met **Technologies**: devices used to ensure compliance with a created norm; include technologies of self **Strategies**: minimal functionalities linking programmes and technologies whose post-hoc identification helps to understand purposes (not) being achieved	1. Forms of visibility, ways of seeing and perceiving 2. Distinctive ways of thinking and questioning, relying on procedures and vocabulary to produce 'truth' 3. Specific ways of acting, intervening and directing, relying on power technologies 4. Ways of forming subjects, selves and persons

'other' creativities, not necessarily those having social or commercial recognition. Hanson (2013) takes a wider view of creativity which could be used to anchor any specific analysis of creativity manifestations in relation to what are the supporting relations that perpetuate creativity as a social construct and as a field of enquiry.

With these insights it is now possible to draw a typology of power relations which could be used by creators to analyse in more depth their attempts to 'balance' their work with their lives, and which could also provide complementary insights to the use of systems ideas in managing creativity. The following are three layers of relations whose interaction could be generating conditions for the emergence of creativities and creative subjects (individual, collective).

1   **Declarations**: These are explicit discourses and associated practices that converge towards the production of ways of structuring individual and collective conduct. Together with bodies of knowledge that emerge in

parallel, these select necessary conducts that are promoted within the social body. Relevant knowledge (including that of the population as a whole) helps in turn devise better ways to monitor and correct human conduct.

2 **Technologies**: These are operationalisations of declarations in the social body that establish specific compliance practices and ways of monitoring such compliance. Operating at both the collective and individual level, they use existing or new practices to set norms and ways to follow them. Technologies here also include those that individuals use on themselves as a result of pursuing a telos through focusing on part of a self that needs work and the establishment of practices on the self to meet the telos.

3 **Functionalities**: These are a posteriori effects of assembling converging declarations and technologies to meet specific purposes. Functionalities are said to be 'ethical' in that they show how individuals or organisations have made use of declarations and technologies, and how such uses can yield limitations and opportunities for exerting counter-conduct at both individual and collective levels of thinking and action.

The operation of these layers of power generates and is influenced by creators' *ethical conducts* as the following figure suggests.

As the figure shows, the suggested *convergence* of declarations, technologies and ethical functionalities for creativity situations does not need to be elucidated or interpreted as another form of alignment as advocated by the systems model of Csikszentmihalyi (1988). In this complementary analysis, *tensions* are to be accepted, and not forced into the direction of success or failure but moved in the best directions that creators foresee as leading to their recreation (Hanson, 2013).

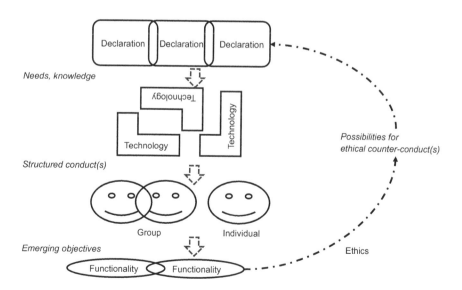

Figure 6.1 A governmentality analytics for creativity

Moreover, the analysis of convergences between these elements and their effects can lead creators to identify how we have become subjects of ethical conducts, and therefore devise and act upon *discerned possibilities for counter-conduct* as we see fit within existing power relations. We could then conceive of our creativity journeys differently, meaning that we could devise our own creativities and bring different ethical values to those being 'nicely' and often unconsciously nudged towards us.

With different ideas about our creativities, we could also devise 'other' systems of enquiry about our creative journeys: We could abide by different values, constraints or activities. Ethical reflection based on governmentality could then complement systems thinking. It could also be that as creators we let go of systems ideas. For myself as a systems thinker, this could be a hard pill to swallow, but an option that deserves to be considered.

Analysis of convergences of well-being, work and balance

In this section, I use the preceding elements of analysis to look back at how my own journey was becoming somehow 'successful' whilst still aiming to achieve a 'balance' as an individual. My aim is to further understand how the convergences noted generated some effects, and how power relations could be used by myself or other creators to redefine ourselves according to how we shape what we perceive as 'the right things to do'.

From the self-ethnography, I could then see that there are several convergent *declarations*. I name only a few given that I choose a boundary for analysis that reinterprets some of the highlighted practices that were denounced in the previous self-ethnography. The reader could expand the analysis by making her own identification of other convergences and their effects on creators like myself.

My work on my own well-being was being echoed at work and elsewhere. In the society where I currently live, there are public declarations by government and organisational policies. Regarding the latter, there is in my organisation an employee assistance programme (EAP) that aims to support workers to enhance well-being through training, attendance at relevant conferences and pursuance of personal development opportunities. To name a few, I have been attending training activities and receiving mentoring, and have also become a mentor. My workplace is currently promoting more attentiveness to health in both staff and students as mentioned in the previous chapter. Mental health of staff and students is deemed to be a key issue in the UK. There is an overall *need* for people and organisations to care about our mental health.

Outside work and as reported earlier, I have become somehow an 'expert user' of mental health services, given that the UK government has issued policies and enabled charities and organisations to provide services and support to those who are (self-)deemed as suffering from some condition: The spectrum of conditions is long and still not fully defined. A recent joint policy between the Departments of Health and Work and Pensions conceives of mental health as something to be managed, given that work absenteeism due to this issue (resulting from work stress) and physical disabilities could be costly for the economy in general (Improving Lives, 2017). Attention, therefore, also aims to put people back in jobs. Hence, we have the connection between job seeking and mental health also mentioned in the self-ethnography chapter.

These and other policies bring some relevant *knowledge*. For example, one in four adults is said to suffer from mental health problems in the UK. Ill health costs the UK economy between 70 and 100 billion pounds per year according to the Annual Report of the UK Chief Medical Officer (Davies, 2013). Existing *knowledge disciplines* like psychology are now including if not extending knowledge about different mental health conditions in both education and practice. Treating such conditions (often with the help of online technologies or mobile applications) could help *health professionals* reveal other conditions and other treatments to be further advanced or created.

In terms of the convergence of *governing technologies*, the preceding and related declarations (i.e. well-being seems to be a new metamorphosis for health management programmes at work and elsewhere) have made use of existing and new ways to empower individuals whilst making us responsible for our health management. In the realm of well-being, creativity can be interpreted as an umbrella construct that involves using therapeutic technologies as described in the self-ethnography (e.g. crafting, walking, mindfulness, self-help groups, mobile apps for mindfulness, self-evaluations, etc.). Often, these target individuals and groups, and operate via a facilitator who could be a figure to whom I and others Foucault, 1988, 1994b. Facilitators themselves could also be considered as subjects of these technologies.

As mentioned earlier, the organisation that I attend provides to its funders 'progress' reports where we assess our own well-being. In similar ways to the meetings between my friend, the career coach and myself, my organisation needs to show to government that recovery goals have been achieved. My friend is now using her relationship with this organisation to show that she is also working on her recovery, so that her government benefits can be maintained.

This is a sort of 'conditional' *welfare* umbrella set of technologies first described by Henman (2010) in his analysis of the implementation and provision of electronic government services in Australia. Through the provision of benefits on condition that progress is being made and recorded, societies could end up segmenting their populations into those who 'meet' such conditions and those who don't, and therefore reinforcing economic and social exclusion.

The type of condition-based funding practice is also spreading to universities and charities. From a governmentality perspective, this practice could also be considered a *technology* to ensure that creativity is to yield some economic benefits (e.g. reintegration to work, entrepreneurship or social enterprising). My own project idea and some 'seed' (internal) funding that I received after being nudged to apply for it require that I submit a project grant proposal. At work, I have been given additional support in the form of information and stakeholder networking sessions. If successful, it will be on me to manage the project to its satisfactory completion. I will be also deemed a successful researcher, with some 'power' to develop my own research agenda. It is expected that I will be able to manage my time to write project bids and meet stakeholders and the like, whilst teaching and supervising increasing numbers of students.

This seems to have become the new 'normal' academic life, which is to be balanced with my 'other' lives.

Elsewhere, my friend could, with some more 'recovery', become employable and then be less expensive to fund in the eyes of the government.

I can also see *other governing technologies* to help me 'succeed'. At work and with my consent, I have been sent to counselling and mentoring sessions. Afterwards, they have asked me if I feel more empowered or confident to deal with stresses at work. I do. I have also felt more *empowered* after being engaged with my well-being activities outside work and reading about or practicing mindfulness, self-acceptance and confidence. I have worked on my stress, identifying its triggers and devising ways to cope with it as described previously.

I know now that I can manage myself more effectively. Through support and empowerment, I have become more self-confident, and I feel happier with myself.

This seems to be an expected and somehow inescapable form of human conduct, leading me to regress to the 'mean' of the 'normal' population (Goldacre, 2003; Dobelli, 2013), something that behavioural economics, another knowledge discipline, has promoted to possibly influence economic policies and human conduct (Thaler, 2009).

The operation of the preceding declarations, technologies and functionalities can be seen in the following diagram.

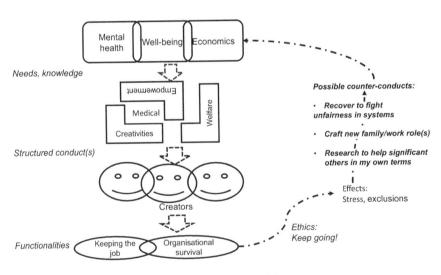

Figure 6.2 A governmentality analysis of a creative life balance

As the diagram shows, in terms of *achieved objectives and emerging functionalities*, the interplay of (mental) health declarations and the use of (creativity, empowerment, welfare) technologies has resulted in several ethical conducts: survival of myself, my significant others (i.e. family) and 'my' organisations (work, etc.). I have been able to continue in my roles as academic, father, expert user and community member. It is up to me to manage some unintended effects (a future setback). I must keep going. Success is elusive.

There could also be other effects derived from governmentalities. The self-ethnography also revealed effects in the ecology of mental health related to new (social) entrepreneurship or volunteer opportunities for expert users. Organisations like the one I attend have set up new services, and the sector seems to be expanding whilst still making use of volunteers.

Following Henman (2010) again, it could be said that government policies and technologies could also generate population exclusions by establishing conditionality. The question to be asked here about this is: Is exclusion an inevitable effect?

In response to this question, it becomes important to pay attention to how, through the promotion of creativities, creators and non-creators could become continuously *marginalised*. My previous work on using systems thinking to promote inclusion in planning (Córdoba-Pachón, 2010) and that of Midgley (2000) would need to be somehow 'rediscovered' in the light of new declarations, technologies (including information technologies) and functionalities that are now being nudged on us in different realms of life (academia, industry, social services).

Because of the aforementioned and on a personal level, I still feel that my life is an unfinished business. Not only is my creative project not 'off the ground' yet (i.e. it has not been funded by an external body yet), I still feel I need to continue working on myself. Although I am continuing to 'obey' by following established forms of conduct, as the preceding diagram suggests, I have begun to devise my own ways of counter-conducting myself within available power relations (Foucault, 1984a, b, 1994a). The following section provides a prelude of my 'private' thinking and acting in this regard, and the next chapter of the book will detail it.

Conducts and counter-conducts: a prelude

If I take the idea of the incompleteness of governing forward, for now I could say that I could use my participation in the different power landscapes that I have come across to my own advantage and potentially to the advantage of others.

In the preceding incomplete set of enterprises, I can still work on redefining myself as a successful individual, *with success being what I decide it is* (Manson, 2016). I could continue working on my well-being so that I could continue crafting my family role as a mediocre, OK person. I could get better at dealing with stress whilst still accepting this is a long journey and letting others know about me.

I could let others do what we all think is right, provided that our collective freedom is not eroded.

Following Ackoff and Rovi (2005), and in consideration of where I am in using the enquiry system to deal with tensions or contradictions in my creativity experiences, I could also use well-being activities to 'recover' and thus fight what I see as unfairness operating in work and mental health systems (knowledge ecologies). I could also use my project to bring together organisations and attempt to influence policy-making as my workplace wants me to do. This would need to be done *on my own terms*, meaning that I do not need to stretch myself to meet expected goals to my own detriment as a human being.

As I see it, there could be different possibilities to redefine myself at work and elsewhere. Just recently I took my twins to a research away day at work: That would have been unthinkable to myself a couple of years ago! On arrival and throughout the day, I got some eyebrows raised, some jokes being cracked by myself and others; the overall effect of the day for me at least was that I could show myself as an individual who has to deal with different types of lives and tensions (children's entertainment included when they cannot be at school or with their mum!). This is now part of my creativities.

As I also think of letting go of some ways to manage my own conduct, I could also decide not to pursue any project, and redefine myself as a non-project active academic and focus more on disseminating my ideas in less demanding publication outlets. I could also pursue more actively my role as a mentor. I could or could not continue engaging with applied systems thinking, creativity and mental health communities without putting my health on the line. I could or could not continue being an expert user.

In contemplating these and other possibilities and tensions, I am more confident that whatever I decide or is decided upon, myself and other people will benefit. In the next chapter I will provide what I consider to be a useful ethics of counter-conduct to help orient myself and others as creators in managing creative possibilities.

Concluding remarks

This chapter has provided an alternative interpretation of how creators could make sense of their attempts to use systems thinking ideas and models in the face of the right things to do. From a slightly different perspective, the criticism of the heroic and 'balanced' if not 'successful' lone genius creator has been revisited and enriched.

The chapter has advanced the argument that a further critical analysis of how creativities unfold is needed to complement the use of systems ideas. From the perspective of governmentality analytics, this unfolding is framed within power relations that contribute to sustaining societal fabrics deemed to be essential to regulating human conduct and fulfilling functions related to keeping or advancing organisational work.

Myself, I could make use of insights into the operation of perceived power relations to find more ethical ways to live, with 'ethical' being what I create within such relations to pursue what I think are the right things to do.

The analysis developed in the chapter has opened possibilities to pursue different links between ethics, systems thinking and creativity. In the process, several questions arise:

*   Could systems thinking be considered a set of governing technologies that contributes to ensuring the fulfilment of societal goals and functions?
*   How could its use in the practice of creativity be managed to avoid potential eroding of creators' and non-creators' freedoms?
*   Could there be a unifying ethics for the use of systems models to advance our understanding and management of creativity situations?

These are questions that require further research. Addressing them fully is outside the scope of this book, although in the remaining two chapters of this book some useful suggestions are offered in this regard.

7 Developing ethics for a creative living

Ethics is closer to wisdom than to reason, closer to understanding what is good than to correctly adjudicating particular situations . . . The self-less 'I' is a bridge between the corporeal body which is common to all beings with nervous systems and the social dynamics in which humans live. My 'I' is neither private nor public alone, but partakes of both.

Varela (1999, pp. 1, 62)

Introduction

The journey of this book has taken us to different places. The use of systems ideas in the form of an enriched enquiry system has helped in the identification of and dealing with several creativities. In the previous chapter and to critically address the issue of doing the right thing that has surfaced throughout the journey, there were key insights about what to do and think in relation to myself. I became aware of the importance of continuously redefining myself and my self-conduct to improve my life and that of others.

It is now time to bring ethics explicitly out of what has been referred to as doing the right thing, now including our conduct of ourselves. Ethics needs to be grounded in ideas that could offer possibilities for further reflection and action. Far from establishing rigid or normative ethics for thinking and acting about creativities or ourselves as creators, the purpose of this chapter is to suggest an intermediate path that could open further possibilities. This can also guide future use and research on systems thinking by helping to continue the dialogue that was proposed at the beginning of the book between creativity and systems thinking.

Referring to the ethics proposed as an intermediate one aims to expand creators' awareness from their own creativities towards other aspects of our lives. From then onwards, we could follow our own paths. There are already ethical stances far more developed than the one proposed in this chapter (Watts, 1951; Varela et al., 1993; Varela, 1999; Wright, 2017). I bring some of these thinkers' ideas to bear through a notion of enactment that could then guide creators. I provide some orientations as a kind of starting point for ethical reflection and action in creativity. With these, creators could then develop what I call ethical closure in the directions that they consider appropriate.

The chapter begins perhaps unexpectedly by bringing a valuable metaphor for creativity in education: that of the shopping mall. Education has not been directly touched upon in this book but has been an essential source of inspiration and practice for my own ideas on creativity and systems thinking. This metaphor helps to elicit some constraints and possibilities to enhance creativity in our living as human beings.

Afterwards, previous systems ideas that were proposed to help creators reconnect with their surroundings are revisited, as they initially offer two relevant orientations to pursue: (1) working on the 'I', and (2) reclaiming failure in creativities to foster creative living. These orientations can help creators integrate their activity with our decisions as to how to live a good life. In addition, an intermediate ethics for living creatively requires working in these two aspects as well as (3) engaging responsibly and openly with others. Using these resulting three orientations, key ethical principles and examples to put them in 'practice' are drawn.

The shopping mall metaphor

My self-ethnography showed one example of how people like myself must continuously face contradictions in an unpredictable and fragmented life. In the face of them, we could become more critical to decide what is right to do. Making decisions is not easy (at least not for me!). We live fast-paced lives that often do not seem to stop.

Even the use of systems thinking could fall short of helping us on these decisions. That is why, myself, I had to resort to governmentality ideas to help me make sense of what was going on with my well-being and my creative project.

In response to this fast pace of life that is being promoted worldwide, many higher educational establishments have established physical and learning environments that more resemble *shopping malls* than any other things in life. As individuals, we normally do not intend to spend much time in a shopping mall except if we allow ourselves to be in a kind of window shopping or consumption mode. We browse through shops, play, watch a movie or eat. Like everyone else, we normally pretend we know what we are to do, the reason for our visit.

It is not difficult to see higher education institutions like shopping malls (Berg and Seeber, 2016). In these institutions, students come and go at different times of the day. They have a timetable. And so do we as academic staff, administrators, industry visitors or any other stakeholder. We operate in time-constrained environments that include car parks, teaching rooms, cafés or libraries. At some point during the day or the week we need to go home, spend time with family, eat a bit more healthily and rest.

Using the terminology of Csikszentmihalyi's systems model of creativity, shopping malls of education could also be meeting places for people who participate in or control domains and fields of knowledge. Education, novelty or creativity could emerge together in these places. My own journey in pursuing a creative project at work has highlighted how as academics we are increasingly under pressure to get projects funded. We borrow ideas and methods from others. In our conversations we quickly become constrained by knowledge conventions and lineages. The shopping mall is asking us to buy and sell ideas quickly, so they can become commercialised and the malls can increase their visibility, capacity and turnover.

It could be argued that there are several governmentalities operating at the same time in the education malls, often collaborating or competing (Foucault, 1978, 1979, 1991; Gordon, 1980). Government policies, visa controls, wellbeing programmes, student experiences and uses of technologies – these and other power relations play a role in shaping how we all think and act. One of the effects is that we feel constrained by time, and thus we need to conduct ourselves in expected ways to help the mall survive, with little time for reflection or solitude (Rose, 2013). How we can deal with reflection becomes an issue worthy of exploration in further research.

Another effect that could be further explored is that although mall stakeholders have different and explicit options to pursue in these environments (different shops to visit in the form of courses and other educational activities), we could all become *rational* and calculative selves, always assessing the costs and benefits involved. In the shopping mall, we all become analytically creative subjects of our own time. Academics must also decide between writing the next paper or research grant, making themselves available to student contact, taking their children to school or recovering from tiredness. Daily, administrators must decide which battle to fight with limited resources, families and health to look after. Students need to make decisions on which activity to prioritise to the detriment of others. Their attendance problems could be seen not as their lack of commitment but instead as over-commitment within and beyond the mall.

The list of detrimental effects of the shopping mall in education and elsewhere could go on. It suffices to mention that Susan Cain (2012), in her exploration of the influence that Western culture plays in the shaping of the extroverted individual personality, finds:

> We tend to forget that there is nothing sacrosanct about learning in large group classrooms, and that we organise students this way not because it is the best way to learn but because it is cost-efficient, and what else would we do with our children while the grown-ups are at work? The purpose of school should be to prepare kids for the rest of their lives, but too often what kids need to be prepared for is surviving the school day itself.
>
> (p. 253)

The metaphor of the shopping mall could also be extended to account for what happens in other settings, including organisations, government or the family. Cost-benefit and analytical thinking, although still used to study creators

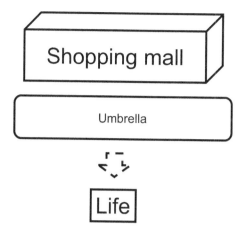

Figure 7.1 Effect of shopping malls

(Sternberg and Lubbart, 1992), is not helping creators or educators develop *ethical wisdom* (Sternberg, 2013). It is providing creators and others with an apparently safe, industry-led and cost-effective *umbrella* that, far from preparing us to face reality, could be isolating us from it.

To contribute to this uncovering of our creativity and our lives, it becomes important to revisit and extend some of the previous ideas of this book.

Another look at the lone genius in creativity

The previous chapters of this book have provided analytical tools that have led me as a creator to reconsider issues of responsibility and balance in creativity. During my self-ethnography, I felt very committed to and almost solely responsible for my creativities (one of them had to do with my own health condition); at work, it is up to me to lead a transdisciplinary team, network with other stakeholders and prepare bids for funding.

As time went by, I felt this journey and myself were entangled in unique if not *heroic* ways. I saw myself as pursuing a greater good, something bigger than me. I could not fail.

From a psychological perspective, Becker (1973) provides a relevant insight into how we as human beings often deny our finite (self-)existence by creating or adhering to what he calls *immortality* projects. He says (p. 212):

> Heroism transmutes the fear of death into the security of self-perpetuation, so much so that people can cheerfully face up to death and even count it under some ideologies . . . if you can be a hero within a communal ideology, then you must be a nagging, whining failure in your family.

This pursuit of heroism often becomes a natural response from our *minds*, which, according to Watts (1951), find it easier to deal with the insecurity of the present moment by clinging to what we can remember from past times or imagine in future ones.

This attitude, mode of thinking and subsequent mode of living could have detrimental consequences for a creator and her significant others:

> When the average person can no longer convincingly perform his safe heroics [transcending or conforming to someone else's standards of life] or cannot hide his failure to be his own hero, then he bogs down [in the denial of creatureliness].
>
> (Becker, 1973, p. 217, brackets added)

A reflection

'I', myself, a 'lone genius', a creator using systems thinking ideas, was trying almost heroically to achieve a balance between my well-being and my other creativities. These ideas helped me realise the impossibility of achieving this goal. It led me to have a setback, to stop and reflect. It led me to seek help in others. Since then my own mindfulness towards myself and my creative project at work has led me to become more aware of the anxious and perfectionist 'I' that could get in the way of being more fully present in my life journey. Saying no also means being able to shift responsibilities to others when needed, and thus escaping the imaginary walls of conduct that shopping malls create for us.

In his later historical analyses of sexuality (1991, 1992), Foucault shows how there were other forms of caring for oneself in Classical and Roman periods of human history. Historically contingent circumstances (e.g. emergence of Christianity) have led to some forms of care becoming sanctioned and more official than others. Fortunately, and following Foucault (1984a), this encouragement could be followed in a different direction as a way of 'heroically obeying' what societies require from us as creators whilst we imagine our present situation and ourselves in different ways.

This same contingency if not serendipity in creativity could make us decide what we can keep and what we can discard in our quests to live a more fulfilling life according to what we think is right for ourselves and others. The quest is to be continuous and is to be lived in the present reality (Foucault 1984a). And that also involves being critical of the use of systems thinking ideas.

The systems model of creativity revisited

Not only the lone genius myth but also the systems model of creativity could contribute to privileging the idea that time and heroism are inevitable constraints. Csikszentmihalyi (1998) regards solitude or too much reflection without action as a potential source of entropy (chaos, disorder, loss of psychic energy) and thus detrimental to creativity. The notion of flow is a neutral one that asks creators to spend time in finding, nurturing and developing their creativity (Csikszentmihalyi, 1998). Although this sounds like an invitation to waste time, the result of flow is a merging of thinking and acting, a standardisation of how these are to be directed, a scientific type of enquiry which in Western society is still deemed as a valuable outcome of education (Dewey, 1910).

As has been claimed throughout this book, it is up to individual creators to rationally find the right balance between their creativities and the rest of their lives by managing perceived contradictions, or to be guided by others in learning to deliberate adequately about what is important to pursue or to be. This becomes an incomplete and governable enterprise. Rather than simply embarking on it, what follows is a proposal to make some ethical sense of it.

Working on the 'I': enactment

During the twentieth century, Watts (1951) was one of the first philosophers to address why we often feel unsatisfied with our lives. He regards the problem of the 'I' as a central problem that contributes to this degree of dissatisfaction. For Watts, we have become used to seeking the confirmation of the existence of an independent and fixed 'I' in every moment of our lives. This idea of the independent 'I' is continuously fuelled by the logical and scientifically oriented mind that has enabled us to analyse, deduce, predict and somehow control the world around us.

Watt's proposal is to let this 'I' and its constant insecurity go. We need to work on ourselves by not paying too much attention to ourselves. Here Watts is linking with Buddhist and other Eastern traditions that regard our dissatisfaction as stemming from wanting reality to be different from what it is (Varela, Thompson and Rosch, 1993; Kabat-Zinn, 2013; Wright, 2017). Working on ourselves becomes a way of reconnecting ourselves with our surroundings, something that was proposed previously in this book and that has been advanced by disciplines like religion.

By combining Eastern and Western perspectives on Buddhism, Wright (2017) provides a middle way to pursue the abandonment of 'I' whilst still using it as a tool for enquiry. For him, through protracted mindful meditation it might be possible to expand awareness on how this 'I' becomes only a part of a bigger universal awareness that could be perceived in everything around us. The aim would be not to 'own' so many feelings, perceptions or thoughts associated with the 'I'. As a result, Wright argues that our awareness and compassion for ourselves and others, as well as a sense of connection with the universe, can be enhanced.

Embedded in developing a more accepting attitude, thinking and acting about the present is the acknowledgement of failure. Like Watts (1951) de Mello (1994) also brings together Western (Christian) and Eastern (Buddhism) thinking traditions to show us how we all wrongly conceive of reality and what we can do about it. For de Mello (1994), we associate the 'I' with the 'me', and the 'me' with failure. Both 'me' and 'failure' are temporary, not worthy of our devotion or clinging to.

The working on the 'I' is therefore neither reality (purposeful success or failure) nor something that is to happen outside it. The interpretations of Puett and Gross-Loh (2016) and Varela (1999) of diverse perspectives from Eastern philosophers (e.g. Confucius, Mencius, Laozi, Zhuangzi, etc.) could also be of value to help us keep this working on the 'I'. Firstly, Puett and Gross-Loh (2016) conceive of reality as fragmented and yet the essential ground for our lives. They encourage creators to develop different ways of seeing and acting in our daily activities. These could include training our heart-minds (senses, reactions, thought and feelings) to refine our responses to others; to play weakness; to reconnect disparate people and things around us; to generate favourable conditions for our and their growth and transformation; and to amplify our learning with the help of or by putting ourselves in the shoes of others.

All these could be achieved with the help of 'artifices' according to Puett and Gross-Loh (2016, p. 169):

> When the mind thinks and is able to act upon its thoughts and move, this is called artifice.

Artifices could be then devised to help us cultivate our minds: They could be a way for us to become creative in our lives. Still, though, there is the question of how far we as creators are willing to go with them and what ethical purposes are to guide our thoughts and actions. Closer to the exploration of random and inter-connected learning as an idea to reconnect creators with their surroundings, it becomes important to also reconnect notions of the 'I' with our own living.

In this regard, Varela (1999) conceives of ethics as inseparable from thinking, cognition and action. This means that we normally *enact* rather than prescribe our ethical behaviour. *Enactment* for Varela means selecting what we consider is relevant for the next moment, depending on previous moments. It is a process that involves our own biology as cognitive beings together with our own living purposes and non-purposes. Varela says:

> In the enactive approach, reality is not a given: it is perceiver-dependent, not because the perceiver 'constructs' it as he or she pleases, but because what *counts* as a relevant world is inseparable from the [cognitive] structure of the perceiver.
>
> (1999, p. 13, original italics, brackets added)

From the preceding quote, Varela's notion of enactment can go beyond purposefully constructed artifices that we could enact to work on the 'I' by worrying less about it. According to Watts (1951) and Varela (1999; Varela et al., 1993) this involves working on abandoning the self-interest and 'street fighter' mentality of the 'I' by accepting that there is no such thing as an 'I' or a 'self', not even in a rational, deliberate or systemic enquiry. This would mean that by working on the 'I', we enrich our experience. *With a broader awareness on the present, the 'self' as we are used to enact it becomes unnecessary for our activity.*

To achieve this, what both Watts and Varela propose is to extend ethical awareness by grounding it in our daily interactions with ourselves and others regardless of our initial assessments. We can learn to notice how we react to situations in the face of breakdowns in our readiness to deal with them by seeking to divide the 'I' from experience. In addition, we can also train ourselves to continue grounding our reactions by learning better ways to enact our interactions with others and the world in general (Varela, 1999; Puett and Gross-Loh, 2016).

This would also mean not only focusing on our purposes to cultivate a selfless 'I'. We also need to allow ourselves to learn from and enter random or non-purposefully oriented situations, as has been proposed earlier in this book. It is expected that love in our relationships with ourselves and others becomes appreciating people and things as they are, without us looking to dissect the 'I' from such appreciations. Love, though, requires practice and hope: practising the abandoning of 'me' in the 'I' whilst hoping this will make us more compassionate with ourselves and others (Watts, 1951; de Mello, 1994; Varela, 1999; Wright, 2017).

As things stand in the use of systems ideas or models for creativity, current binding to reason-led norms about how flow is to be achieved or what the right thing to do is – which I have adopted until now and which Varela (1999) would call morality instead of ethics – seems to have contributed to isolating or limiting the potential of creativities to be lived beyond specific domains or fields of knowledge. With enacting as linking what we do with how we live or even how reflect on our lives, creativity becomes less becoming and more being, doing, thinking, living in the present and accounting for what is really 'not' there and could be. De Mello (1994, p. 78) says:

> To acquire happiness, you do not have to do anything, because happiness cannot be acquired. Does anybody know why? Because we have it already . . . Then why don't you experience it? Because you have to drop something. You have got to drop illusions . . . your ambitions, your greed, your cravings.

For some advocates of the systemic nature of creativity, this notion of enactment could be just a rehearsing of what they have said all along: that creativity is about adaptation and that it is about evolution in life (Barron, 1972; Montuori and Purser, 1995; Montuori, 2017). However, what Varela provides is an alternative and somehow paradoxical route to this realisation, one which takes a detour and stops by encouraging creators to work on the 'I' of themselves and doing it in what seem to be non-purposeful ways.

This 'stop' is being recognised by Csikszentmihalyi (1996) and Langer (2014) only as a subsidiary for the notions of flow and mindfulness respectively, and without transcending too much the boundaries that they set out for what they consider creativity to be or how to develop it. Varela's account of how we can connect knowledge with living (1999) inverts and expands on these relationships by recognising ethics in the wider context of our biological lives, in how we could study creativity or in how we could make our lives richer beyond using scientifically accepted ideas, methods or technologies. These could still be used to help us live in the present rather than making us feel or believe that we can confound responsibility with isolation or blame, or predict or control the future from a distance (Watts, 1951).

Enactment could also provide *closure* on the idea that Foucault has proposed on self as a continuous project or work of 'art' (Foucault, 1984a; Varela, 1999). With a common connection established between ethics and cognition, creators like myself could make sense of both creativity and ourselves. For myself, closure also means that even with systems thinking ideas informing creativity, there is something bigger than creativity or knowledge. This something bigger is my own life, which I need to live with a bit more awareness than is currently the case and without subordinating it fully to 'higher' purposes: I still need to live my life.

Insights from using the notion of enactment to work on our 'I's could also help us accept these 'I's that influence and are influenced by our creativities, so that we also accept *and* engage with reality despite us not really grasping or agreeing with it:

> There is no explanation you can give that would explain away all the sufferings and evil and torture and destruction and hunger in the world! You will never explain it . . . Because life is a mystery, which means your thinking mind cannot make sense out of it . . . you have got to wake up and then you will suddenly realise that reality is not problematic, you are the problem.
>
> (de Mello, 1994, p. 86)

Engaging openly and responsibly with the present

In her exploration of random and inter-connected learning, Mary Catherine Bateson (1994) talks about change and continuity in a situation as unfolding in two different layers of interaction, "one flowing under or over or within the other, at different levels of abstraction: superficial change within profound continuity, and superficial continuity within profound change" (p. 89). Creativity as a medium and outcome could be moulded on the idea of balancing the novel with the same, the purposeful with the purposeless, as has been hinted at previously in this chapter.

If we as creators are to extend creativity to different realms of life, as seems to be the case per my own self-ethnography, it becomes relevant then to accept that our openness and responsibility with 'others' and our surroundings is not fully under our own control. In other words, we can engage randomly with and through creativity in what could be regarded as open, continuous interactions with the present. From a governmentality perspective, serendipitous or (un) purposeful engagement can be regarded as an incomplete set of enterprises. Efforts invested in creating something valuable, novel and legitimately conducted could also be conceived of as resulting from counter-conducts.

This consideration could on the one hand help promote societal values like perseverance and dealing with contradiction. On the other hand, it also opens opportunities to go back and change our minds, ourselves and the surroundings that we live in, at work and elsewhere.

The idea of openness, randomness and responsibility in creative engagement could thus be taken forward as well as backward when we engage creatively with our knowledge enterprises. When navigating knowledge ecologies, if creators think that they must respect convention or tradition (Abbott, 2004), or master previous knowledge as the only path available to advance it or widen the impact of their creativity (Csikszentmihalyi, 1996), they might like to consider this again.

There is the opportunity to revisit knowledge and see it as historically contingent and in need of being sifted through, as Foucault suggests. For the fields of creativity or systems thinking, this could also mean being able to transcend existing boundaries that have been drawn to make them rationally or logically oriented, and include ideas of other fields (metaphysics, quantum physics or religion) (Khisty, 2010).

As Watts (1951) puts it (and Wright 2017 aims to further this claim by comparing evolutionary psychology with Buddhism), scientific fields might not fully need non-scientific fields to logically prove their own theories or ideas; however, mankind needs *both* to make sense of one's own life and relationships with reality (Ibid):

> For 'Christ' [God, the universe or similar] stands for the reality that there is no separate [i.e. scientifically validated] self to surrender . . . 'Christ' is the realization that there is no separate 'I'. 'I' do nothing for myself . . . I and the Father are one.
>
> (brackets added)

For the use of the systems model of creativity, transcending existing boundaries means that although we do not entirely forget previous engagements, there is an opportunity to recreate relations between creators, domains of knowledge and fields, to borrow and redefine ideas, to even redraw existing lineages of knowledge or reimagine ourselves as belonging to not yet established settlements or disciplines. As this book has shown so far, inclusion of 'other' systems and non-systems thinking oriented ideas has proved fruitful to help creators. We might need to let go of the fear to control complexity or to provide reasonable grounds to ethically guide creators. Doing so could open further opportunities for the use of systems models and for future dialogues between creators and others, as the final chapter of this book will propose.

Engagement should not stop there. Not only knowledge but our lives keep flowing very dynamically. For myself as a creator, a challenge is to let myself engage with other people from whom I know I can learn about life, not only about potential research projects. If there is anything like a career, I could accept more openly that mine has been and is pretty undefined at times, perhaps with the exception of systems thinking.

Overall, it can be said that promoting open (and random) as well as responsible engagement in creativity could help us shift existing umbrellas from the malls that we inhabit in our lives, and to engage differently and systemically with things 'out there'. Yes, there could be risks and uncertainty. There could be 'shit' and 'serendipity'. There needs to be responsibility. There could be creativity. And there could be life.

Towards an ethics for systems-based creativity

With the aforementioned ideas and considering working on the 'I' whilst welcoming these features of creativity and life, I now proceed to propose the following orientations to help myself and other creators have some closure and openings about living creative lives.

I also consider the resulting 'ethical system' one which could help us become 'anonymous', given that this is how I have experienced my journey into creativity. The orientations could be conceived of as overlapping with each other and helping creators to enhance not only our creativities but also other realms of our lives.

The orientations are:

1   **Self-cultivation**. We need to cultivate ourselves by continuously observing, understanding and accepting the 'I' within ourselves. To do so, we could become a bit more mindful, slower, introverted, solitary or mediocre. We could just take ourselves lightly whilst we think we are part of the universe.
2   **Reclaiming failure**. The world we live in is fragile, contradictory, unjust and difficult to live in, but it is the best we have now. Even within failure, we still have some available freedom within and beyond the governmentalities that make us what we are. If creativity is temporarily 'lived' (Pope, 2005), why don't we try to fail as many times as possible?
3   **Encouraging open and responsible engagement with the present**. Whether we like it or not, it is better to become friends with our 'I's and the world around us whilst we devise ways to positively transform if not integrate both, in the face of serendipity and 'shit'.

These orientations could then help us in our quest to see creativity as a system as initially proposed in chapter 2 of this book. The following is an updated diagram from that chapter. We can use the orientations to help us to creatively deal with life. Failure (or success) is just a small part of life we could reclaim rather than depend on.

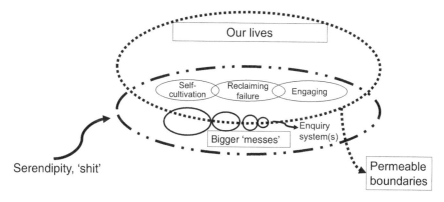

Figure 7.2 Ethical orientations for a creative living in the present

These orientations could inform what we think and what we do as creators. Some examples of their application are now offered with the intention to yield some further insights into how we can help advance our creativity and that of the people we work with or relate to.

Some examples

The following examples are presented under a specific orientation; however, they could link to the other ones as a *system*, as life links things together without us knowing it.

Self-cultivation

I now know that I tend to overestimate myself. I was brought up not to fail, to always succeed. This often gets me into trouble. I can become arrogant and distant, anxious, extremely competitive and, why not, jealous. I am now applying some compassion to myself. When feeling anxiety, lack of self-confidence or sadness, I try to see why that is. I know I am very harsh on myself. I am learning to soothe myself in adequate ways. So I try to talk about feelings. I try to give myself a spiritual hug. I am now more able to share these feelings, and listen to others, including mentors. I am now valuing them more than I used to. It is OK to be introverted and want to spend time alone.

I need to be careful when entering into the rivers of imagination, work and parenting. I know this. With too much immersion in these I feel drained, anxious and miserable, not good enough. I am now doing a bit more swimming during the week and looking after my diet. These I know help me stay physically healthy. I continue going to my self-help groups. I keep drawing my mandalas, writing funny short stories, reading fiction, watching movies and sleeping in the office when tired. The recovery journey is a long one for me.

Talking about my feelings is important. I am also more accepting of the idea that inevitably I will have crap days when I will feel like a complete failure. I am working to accept them.

I can see that writing this book and pursuing other creative ideas are good enough. I still fear for the future. However, I am doing a bit better at accepting and enjoying life as it is now. I am beginning to appreciate my age. Career wise, I am beginning to feel more OK than was the case before. I am not where sometimes I feel I want to be (that is not clear yet!), but overall, I am valuing myself and my own life more.

Reclaiming failure

A boring workshop

Today I am teaching a workshop (practical session) on quantitative methods for business and management. The students and I are tired. So, I decide to have a small ice breaking activity: some breathing followed by a quick introduction to the workshop and another exercise – laughing at failure. I learned this latter one from attending improv comedy workshops (Goldie, 2015).

For this I ask students to say a word that connects with a previous one (said by me or other students). If they don't do this quickly we all shout 'Fail!' and applaud at the 'failed' individual. When I ask students how they feel about this, some of them are still confused, whilst others say that it felt 'good' to fail.

At some point during the session, I ask students if they like statistics. Some of them say that they hate it! I say that I don't like them either; we just need to become friends with statistics. I tell them what I do to learn statistics: Take some breaks, watch YouTube videos and ask for help. I try to practice bits now and then.

Despite the overall positive feedback at the end of this course, I feel like a failure when teaching statistics. I ask students for help to improve attendance at the workshops. Some of them come up with very creative ideas: having a bed that rolls them from their accommodation to their classrooms; having flexible attendance so if they miss their session they could attend another one (there are several sessions during the week); having a mobile application that reminds them of the sessions they are to attend. More radical solutions include punishing or rewarding attendance by linking it to the final mark, or avoiding block sessions (3 hours) during lunch time. I say these are more radical because I know that their implementation would have to overcome institutional barriers and culture.

Bad days

Yes, there are bad days when I feel like 'crap'. I need to manage my frustration. Things do not happen overnight. I need to learn to leave it to others to do their bit. I often feel as if I 'invest' too much of my time in helping others.

I need to learn how to borrow ideas more carefully and draw boundaries around myself. I know some triggers of my anxiety/frustration/failure – overwork, exceeding expectations.

At work

I have failed as an outstanding academic. I cannot do everything well. I have spoken to the powers that be. I need to be kinder with myself. That, I think, could benefit not only myself but my colleagues, students, family and friends.

Sorry guys, I have failed. I want to be more mediocre now.

Open and responsible engagement(s)

An engaging course

Smart cities are a phenomenon that involves technological, environmental and social considerations. Many universities or educational institutions are based in or near cities whose councils and innovation hubs or clusters strive to promote economic growth.

In a course of creativity, sustainable development or innovation, management education students could be set a project to look at cities they have access to and work in groups of no more than four. The aim would be to come up with one or two sound suggestions to help cities address relevant issues.

If tutors think it is a good idea, the systems concept could be introduced to students – first at a personal level so that students can map all the issues that they have at a time in realising their personal goals at university and beyond. Students could draw a systems map with relations between issues and ask themselves about how their goals could emerge out of the interaction between issues. They could also reflect on temporarily including or marginalising issues and people from their map, so that their issues and goals become more connected, focused and related to wider or bigger issues and (societal) goals.

Group maps of smart city issues could be developed alongside individual maps and discussed with tutors in informal or formal encounters. City stakeholders could be invited to attend group presentations and give their feedback. As is often the case, city councils lay out and make publicly available online their plans to improve life in their cities. These could be used by groups to help them diagnose although not fully copy existing city issues and make their suggestions sounder when presenting them to city stakeholders.

This course has seen several reincarnations. It was initially a postgraduate course on complex decision making using systems thinking. Due to pressures to abandon it, it then became an undergraduate course on creativity and problem solving. After other pressures, it has become a course on creative process management. I keep failing, arguing and persevering.

In class, we could help ourselves to face failure. Practical improv comedy exercises could be used to discover how we face failure and laugh about it (Goldie, 2015); failure can be laughable! We could be protecting our own idea of ourselves as successful, fearful, insecure or human, for which there might not be a need in a creativity course! In class, we could spend some time talking about our own fears, limitations and braveries when coming to and leaving the shopping malls we all feel trapped in. We could talk about how we have become the people we have become and carve some possible ideas to rework our identities. We could help each other with some advice and feedback on our class projects but also on our career plans. We could then go and enjoy coffee, enjoy the present moment and enjoy life as it is.

A project and 'other' ideas that might (not) happen

I continue working on my project to evaluate technology support to help increase employ-ability in people with some mental health conditions. I cannot be a super academic who does everything well. I take responsibility for the success or failure in getting funding for my project. I understand the pressures on my institution and on myself to get funding. I try to keep relationships with stakeholders going. I try to keep on top of my marking of students' work, writing up ideas and papers and submitting research bids. I try.

   I also keep thinking of other and possibly less successful ideas. It is part of whom I am and whom I want to become.

Concluding remarks

From the journey that has been previously described in this book, this chapter has laid out ethical orientations to encourage myself and creators to pursue living a more creative life. A metaphor of the 'mall' was used to generate aware-ness of the importance of unpacking creativity and taking it beyond what we as creators and individuals become used to in our education and our lives in gen-eral. This metaphor could be extended to account for our contradictions in life.

   Given the opportunity to expand our creativities, the notion of *enactment* has been proposed to ground an ethics for creative living. This notion could make us more aware of whom we are at every moment of our lives and help us to decide on whom we could be in relation to reality as we live it. From this notion of enactment, three different orientations (self-cultivation, reclaim-ing failure, promoting open and responsible engagement) have been proposed. These orientations shed some light on some possibilities that were drawn upon to counteract potential detrimental effects of creativities. Some 'specific' whilst overlapping examples derived from them were provided to help me make sense of what I am doing currently about my creativities and what I could also be pursuing in the never-ending enterprise of recreating myself.

   The orientations could also inspire further research in the use of systems thinking to creativity research and practice. To this end, the final chapter of the book provides a summary of the journey and some possibilities to continue dialogues between creativity and systems thinking whatever the present and the future bring to all of us.

8 Final reflections

Can man's intelligence and creativity – his consciousness, indeed, take the giant step necessary to keep up with his technology?
— Frank Barron, 1972, "Towards an Ecology of Consciousness", *Inquiry* (15), pp. 1–4

Introduction

This chapter rounds up the journey of this book. A dialogue was initially established and then further developed between creativity and systems thinking. Systems models have helped take the journey to our lives and to how we can live them more creatively and ethically.

However, systems models like Csikszentmihalyi's or the enquiry system proposed to complement it could be conceived of as *governing technologies* that ourselves or others use to guide our conduct – and as the preceding quote suggests, technologies that we need to keep up with.

As creators, we could do with continuing dialoguing if we are going to make sense of using systems thinking and creativity for our benefit and that of humankind. For the future, the dialogue could be enhanced by taking stock of what has been achieved and how systems thinking and creativity could continue talking to each other.

This chapter is structured in two sections: a first one of *enacted dialogue* that provides a summary of the main insights obtained through the journey; and a second one of enacting dialogue that suggests some further possibilities to keep the dialogue going.

The enacted dialogue so far

This book started by considering the field of knowledge of creativity as a mess, one which is continuously stirred with contributions from established and less established disciplines, or other bodies of knowledge, all of which have lineages and conventions about knowledge. A look at the history of creativity has suggested that despite this field claiming a degree of distinctiveness from others, there are many opportunities to look at creativity as both an individually and collectively based phenomenon. Initially these opportunities were bound within this mess and considered some unchallenged assumptions: Creativity is what socially counts as creative, and studying it requires using models or methods already established (including Csikszentmihalyi's systems model of creativity).

The dialogue thus became a supporting whilst critical one, in particular of the systems ideas and models already present and being used in the creativity field. The addition of complexity theory to support systemic thinking in creativity was a partial if not binding solution to creators' dealing with the contradictions and tensions encountered when pursuing our ideas.

An alternative to this potential limitation of systems thinking in creativity was brought from the applied systems thinking field/body of knowledge. In this field, the systems idea is used to enquire about situations, and to use other ideas to help people deal with contradictions, tensions and the complexity of such situations. These contradictions could be lived individually or collectively in the Western enterprise of advancing (sadly not rediscovering) knowledge.

The dialogue continued by proposing and enriching an enquiry system (another model) to help creators. Enquiry was also supported with a knowledge-based perspective that could explain in more detail how creativity happens in academic and other settings that worldwide are currently under pressure to deliver value for money, whatever this means.

Then the dialogue became more of a reflective monologue through a self-ethnography that revealed how there could be not only one but several ideas about creativity, some of which connect creators with ourselves. The monologue became again a dialogue, not only between systems thinking and creativity but also with knowledge ecologies of mental health and employment, and later more widely with societal governmentalities that emerge and operate in the social body to guide our conduct individually or collectively.

This extended dialogue gave me the opportunity and challenge to face up to the issue of doing the right thing, an issue that became a journey companion from the start and which now helps me connect my creativities with the rest of my life. I have extended the dialogue to creators, other individuals and their whole lives so that we can all think of living better lives than is currently the case.

Enacting future dialogues

As individuals and whether we like it or not, we cannot remain isolated from the Western enterprise of advancing knowledge through science. This enterprise has provided valuable benefits to individuals and organisations. In the social science realm, it has been through research in creativity that it is now possible to argue that more appropriate environments are needed if creativity is to flourish. If it was not for this enterprise, we would not have seen the light of the creativity field.

The journey of enacting an extended dialogue between creativity and systems thinking has also revealed a bigger journey, onto which I now invite the reader. It is the journey to involve others from these and other bodies of knowledge to participate. The enterprise of advancing knowledge is, by its very own definition and considering it part of societal governmentalities, an incomplete one. Creators and their supporting advocates, groups or communities could benefit from this dialogue. The dialogue does not need to arrive at some intended point. It just needs to continue, even if this means rediscovering knowledge and its dynamics between those engaged in it.

This book therefore provides a rediscovery of ideas of both systems thinking and creativity. Within this rediscovery there could be several possibilities to promote future dialogue, and I invite the reader to borrow them. The following possibilities could serve as a starting point:

Exploring and borrowing from other lineages in creativity

Using the ideas of Abbott, creativity could be creative about itself. In this book and using these ideas, two main lineages were defined and used to contribute to the systems model of creativity of Csikszentmihalyi and followers. But there could be more. A creative historian of creativity could then explore how the systems model came to be; what other associations between systems and creativity could have been established; and how debates between different approaches of socio-culturally oriented and progressively oriented creativity have benefitted and marginalised groupings operating within or across disciplines. The survival of these groups could be contrasted with the survival of others.

From this, a creative historian could also 'borrow' stories from other fields; she could translate those stories into ones that could appeal to the conventions of the creativity field; she could also venture to propose existing or new stories to help this field to continue exploring its own 'maze' using different and (why not) creative routes or paths.

Enhancing experience within and beyond creativity

As an academic researcher, throughout this journey I have found myself in need of *unlearning* analytical thinking and incorporating *experience*, something that could be initially seen as 'mundane' or 'inconsequential' but that has given me an opportunity to redefine myself as a creator.

In this regard, the creativity field could help applied systems thinking to rediscover, regain and shift its analytical-methodological focus. The use of systems ideas to advance creativity could become more *experiential*, and from the standpoint not only of stakeholders but of creators or facilitators ourselves.

The notion of *enactment* covered in this book could help us to become more aware of what we bring to our own creativity situations and how we become subjects of forms of conduct. Experiences could help us cultivate more the 'I' and less the (goal oriented) 'me' as de Mello (1994) has suggested. Such experiences could be nurtured in random encounters with situations where we have not planned to do anything. The experience of facing the unexpected (which advocates of complexity seem to aim to tame by making the experiences 'safe' for learning) could be also included in our efforts to come to terms with the fluid nature of what constitutes our 'self'.

And what is more, both creativity and systems thinking could continue talking together to find ways to bring diverse human experiences (including those of teachers and students) to the classroom and the workplace. This should be done with the purpose of not only getting students an economically viable job so that our institutions can claim better employability (Robinson and Aronica, 2015), but *also* allowing them to find their own 'I's, to fail and learn from doing so, to go where they want and do not want to be, to fully enact their lives, even if that means abandoning the goals that they and us set out initially to achieve.

Therefore, more mindful and inter-connected learning is needed in the classroom. As educators in creativity and life in general, we need to continue breaking the silos that are now being built by (higher) education malls. We need to bring surrounding communities to universities. We need to make *marginalisation* a key problem to be explored in our courses.

To support the preceding goals, we would need to rediscover knowledge via different routes in what Abbott (2001) has called the 'maze' in social science and bring along those who might have been left out when we have tried to find the most efficient but not necessarily most inclusive routes to knowledge. This is also creativity, perhaps not as novel or publishable as we know it, but valuable and relevant to others.

Adding complexity to the 'I'

Adding the aforementioned challenges and complexities as well as complexity theory to creativity needs to consider the attributes of 'shit', 'serendipity', 'failure', 'responsibility', 'governmentality' and others that could be elicited from reflecting on our own journeys as creators, educators, fathers, mothers or other family members.

In the maze of social science, there could still be unexplored routes. Systems thinking and complexity ideas have much to offer to other settlements or disciplines of knowledge. So far and to the best of my knowledge, complexity ideas have been included in systems thinking at a more collective and prescriptive level, to the potential disregard of the individual. Individuals are complex and unpredictable. This possibility for dialoguing with other disciplines could also bring together individuals from psychology, neuroscience, management and other fields to try to understand better how different levels of analysis within the 'I' could come together to help creators self-cultivate and engage if not rediscover ways of dealing with contradictions and tensions.

For researchers in creativity and systems thinking, this could also mean perhaps rediscovering old ideas and friends as well as foes. But if we accept that we cannot fully manage the world around us, neither what constitutes serendipity, success, 'shit' or failure, then rediscovery becomes a risk worth taking.

Talking to our (mental) health(s) and to others dealing with them

This journey has revealed valuable insights into the realities of mental health in conjunction with the other realities of daily life. The self-ethnography has invited the reader to consider how creativity is being used in such realities, and how it needs to be carefully if not critically and continuously crafted. The systemic nature of mental health has also been highlighted. Future dialogues between disciplines, practices and mental health could consider how ideas about success need a wider view of their effects in individuals and those supporting us. Systems thinking could continue playing a role in helping people plan and evaluate services across organisations to support those with mental health conditions. The role(s) of technologies would need also to be explored in relation to wider ideas about health and success.

Finally, three bedtime stories

We should not forget that in both creativity and systems thinking, serendipity, society and life ultimately define what the next moment for us to live is. Should we then succumb to our blindness and that of others? Or should we keep trying, with the knowledge that lady luck might or might not favour us? Should we keep the ideal that we are progressing in our quest for being or becoming creative whilst still struggling to get out of going in circles? Or should we still put faith in our institutions and their practices, their ways of thinking and working, which could end up undermining our motivations and draining our energy?

We should not forget our own human condition, the present moment that is all we have and the love and compassion that are required at each and every moment with ourselves, others and the rest of the universe.

a   Simple worries

Dear children:

For you at this age your only worries seem to be about attending your friends' parties, skipping school, eating cakes and ice creams, picking up insects and getting what you want when you want it.

I have noticed that if these things do not happen you can get upset. You will not give up in asking for them!

In your minds, there does not seem to be room for anything else. You focus your full attention on something. I wish I could do the same.

You do not seem to worry about uncertainty. You feel fear of things you can get scared of, but also you marvel at new discoveries. You do not hesitate in asking for support or asking questions when you need to.

What a wonderful age.

b   Walking through the fog

Dear children:

Time flies by! It is now a new year, and you have turned 4 years of age!

Still remember our Christmas walk at your uncle's place. Next day after arrival we all ventured to explore the neighbourhood.

It was a foggy morning, and I felt lost as I could not find my bearings. But you kept going. For you it was the novelty of being in a foreign country and seeing your cousins for the first time which made the walk a wonderful experience. It was us, the adults, who kept drawing comparisons between here and there.

We managed to keep up with you and finally made it back to the house all in one piece. Perhaps this is what creativity and life are about – to be adventurous, to keep connections, to find ways of communing despite feeling lost or isolated at times.

Your curiosity and lack of fear keep me going!

c   A day

Dear children:

Part of my job involves travelling. The whole of my job involves thinking. Sometimes even if I am with you my mind is elsewhere!

I would love to wake up in the morning and spend time playing with you. Then get ready, drop you at school and tour around local places, speak to people and discuss ideas. I could then land at a desk or in a nice café to do some writing and thinking. And I could continue touring around or just go to the office to let my mind rest.

I would love to know that you are experiencing the world as it is when in school. You keep telling me about the things you learn. They do not make much sense yet to me, but I still love to hear them!

Please be a little patient; I am not the young person I used to be. If I am not energetic enough for you and you get desperate, please help me get through the day.

Often and unexpectedly, life throws things at us for which we are not prepared.

Let us try to spend the day in the best way we can.

You and I, your mum, the neighbours, our friends and families, my students and colleagues, those who are ill and even those we do not know, we are all trying to live this day.

Just be grateful for this day, a day.

I am now letting go of this journey to where it wants to continue, with or without me.

References

Abbott, A., 1988. *The System of Professions: An Essay on the Division of Expert Labour.* Chicago: University of Chicago Press.

Abbott, A., 2001. *Chaos of Disciplines.* Chicago: University of Chicago Press.

Abbott, A., 2004. *Methods of Discovery: Heuristics for the Social Sciences.* New York: W. W. Norton and Company Inc.

Abbott, A., 2005. Linked ecologies: States and universities as environments for professions. *Sociological Theory,* 23(3), pp. 245–274.

Abbott, A., 2012. The vicissitudes of methods. *International Journal of Social Research Methodology Lecture – 5th Social Science Research Methods Festival.* St Catherine's College, University of Oxford, Oxford, UK: National Centre for Research Methods and Economic and Social Research Council (ESRC). [online] Available at: <www.youtube.com/watch?v=v1I665VBe4A> [Accessed August 2018].

Ackoff, R.L., 1978. *The Art of Problem Solving.* New York: John Wiley and Sons.

Ackoff, R.L., 1981. *Creating the Corporate Future: Plan or Be Planned for.* New York: John Wiley and Sons.

Ackoff, R.L. and Rovin, S., 2005. *Beating the System: Using Creativity to Outsmart Bureaucracies.* San Francisco: Berrett-Koehler Publishers Inc.

Amabile, T., 1998. How to kill creativity. *Harvard Business Review,* September-October, pp. 77–87.

Amabile, T. and Kramer, S., 2011. *The Progress Principle: Using Small Wins to Ignite Joy, Engagement and Creativity at Work.* Boston (US): Harvard Business Review Press.

Barron, F., 1968. *Creativity and Personal Freedom.* London: D. Van Nostrand Company Inc.

Barron, F., 1972. Towards an ecology of consciousness. *Inquiry,* 15(1–4), pp. 95–113.

Barron, F., 1997. *Introduction.* In Barron, F., Montuori, A. and Barron, A, *Creators on Creating.* New York: Jeremy P. Tarcher/Penguin, pp. 1–21.

Barron, F., Montuori, A., and Barron, A., 1997. *Creators on Creating: Awakening and Cultivating the Imaginative Mind.* New York: Jeremy P. Tarcher/Penguin.

Bateson, G., 1972. *Steps to an Ecology of Mind.* Chicago: University of Chicago Press.

Bateson, G., 1979. *Mind and Nature.* London: Flamingo (Fontana Paperbacks).

Bateson, M.C., 1994. *Peripheral Visions: Learning Along the Way.* New York: Harper.

Bateson, M.C., 2006. The double bind: Pathology and creativity. *Cybernetics and Human Knowing,* 12(1–2), pp. 11–21.

Becker, E., 1973. *The Denial of Death.* London: Souvenir Press.

Berg, M. and Seeber, B., 2016. *The Slow Professor: Challenging the Culture of Speed in the Academy.* Toronto: University of Toronto Press.

Bostrom, N., 2016. *Superintelligence: Paths, Dangers, Strategies.* Oxford: Oxford University Press.

Cain, S., 2012. *Quiet: The Power of Introverts in a World that Can't Stop Talking.* New York: Penguin.

Canthoper, T., 2012. *Depressive Illness: The Curse of the Strong.* 3rd edition. London: Sheldon Press.

Chambers, C., 2017. *The Seven Deadly Sins of Psychology: A Manifesto for Reforming the Culture of Scientific Practice.* Princeton (US): Princeton University Press.

Chapman, J., 2002. *System Failure: Why Governments Must Learn to Think Differently.* London: Demos Institute.

Checkland, P., 1981. *Systems Thinking, Systems Practice.* Chichester: John Wiley and Sons.

Checkland, P. and Scholes, J., 1990. *Soft Systems Methodology in Action.* Chichester: John Wiley and Sons.

Churchman, C.W., 1968. *The Systems Approach.* New York: Dell Publishing.

Córdoba-Pachón, J.R., 2009. Trans-disciplinary collaboration and information systems. In: Cock, N., ed. *E-Collaboration: Concepts, Methodologies, Tools and Applications.* Hershey, PA: IGI Global, pp. 1501–1509.

Córdoba-Pachón, J.R., 2010. *Systems Practice in the Information Society.* London: Routledge

Córdoba-Pachón, J.R., 2011. Embracing human experience in applied systems thinking. *Systems Research and Behavioral Science,* 28(6), pp. 680–688.

Córdoba-Pachón, J.R., Pilkington, A., and Bernroider, E., 2012. Information systems as a discipline in the making: Comparing EJIS and MISQ between 1995 and 2008. *European Journal of Information Systems,* 21(5), pp. 479–495.

Córdoba-Pachón, J.R. and Robson, W., 2005. *What Method Suits Collaborative Research?* Research Memorandum 49. Hull, UK: Hull University Business School.

Cropley, A., 2001. *Creativity in Education and Learning: A Guide for Teachers and Educators.* London: Routledge.

Cropley, A., 2006. In praise of convergent thinking. *Creativity Research Journal,* 18(3), pp. 391–404.

Csikszentmihalyi, M., 1988. Society, culture and person: A systems view of creativity. In: Csikszentmihalyi, M., ed. *The Systems Model of Creativity: The Collected Works of Mihaly Csikszentmihalyi.* Dordrecht: Springer, pp. 47–61.

Csikszentmihalyi, M., 1996. *Creativity: Flow and the Psychology of Discovery and Invention.* New York: Harper Collins.

Csikszentmihalyi, M., 1998. *Aprender a Fluir (Finding Flow).* Barcelona: Editorial Kairos.

Csikszentmihalyi, M., 1999a. Implications of a systems perspective for the study of creativity. In: Sternberg, R., ed. *Handbook of Creativity.* Cambridge: Cambridge University Press, pp. 313–335.

Csikszentmihalyi, M., 1999b. If we are so rich, why aren't we happy? *American Psychologist,* 54(10), pp. 821–827.

Csikszentmihalyi, M. and Getzels, J., 1971. Discovery-oriented behaviour and the originality of creative products: A study with artists. *Journal of Personality and Social Psychology,* 19(1), pp. 47–52.

Csikszentmihalyi, M. and Wolfe, R., 2000. New conceptions and research approaches to creativity: Implications of a systems perspective on creativity education. In: Heller, K.A., Monks, F.J., Sternberg, R., and Subotnik, R., eds. *International Handbook of Giftedness and Talent.* London: Elsevier, pp. 81–93.

Davies, S., 2013. *Chief Medical Officer Annual Report 2013: Public Mental Health Priorities – Investing in the Evidence.* [online] Available at: <www.gov.uk/government/publications/chief-medical-officer-cmo-annual-report-public-mental-health> [Accessed April 2018.]

De Mello, A., 1994. *Despierta! (Awareness) – Charlas Sobre la Espiritualidad.* Bogotá: Editorial Norma.

Dean, M., 2010. *Governmentality: Power and Rule in Modern Society.* London: Sage.

Denzin, N., 2012. *Interpretive Autoethnography*. London: Sage.

Dewey, J., 1910. *How We Think*. Mineola; New York: Dover Publications Inc.

Dewey, J., 1910. *How we Think*. New York: Dover Publications Inc.

Dobelli, R., 2013. *The Art of Thinking Clearly*. London: Sceptre.

Dolan, P., 2015. *Happiness by Design*. London: Penguin.

Eagleman, D., 2015. *The Brain: The Story of You*. London: Canongate.

Flood, R.L. and Jackson, M.C., 1991. Total systems intervention: A practical face to critical systems thinking. *Systems Practice*, 4(3), pp. 197–213.

Foucault, M., 1978. Governmentality. In Burchell, G., Gordon, C., and Miller, P., eds. *The Foucault Effect: Studies in Governmentality*. Chicago: University of Chicago Press, pp. 87–104.

Foucault, M., 1979. *Omnes et Singulatim: Towards a Criticism of Political Reason*. The Tanner Lectures on Human Values, Stanford University, February 10 and 16, 1979. [online] Available at: <http://bit.ly/1cXdQrc> [Accessed April 2018.]

Foucault, M., 1982a. The subject and power. *Critical Inquiry*, 8, pp. 777–795.

Foucault, M., 1982b. On the genealogy of ethics: An overview of work in progress. In: Rabinow, P., ed. *The Foucault Reader: An Introduction to Foucault's Thought*. London: Penguin, pp. 340–372.

Foucault, M., 1984a. What is enlightenment? In: Rabinow, P., ed. *The Foucault Reader: An Introduction to Foucault's Thought*. London: Penguin, pp. 32–50.

Foucault, M., 1984b. Politics and ethics: An interview. In: Rabinow, P., ed. *The Foucault Reader: An Introduction to Foucault's Thought*. London: Penguin, pp. 373–380.

Foucault, M., 1984c. What is an author? In: Rabinow, P., ed. *The Foucault Reader: An Introduction to Foucault's Thought*. London: Penguin, pp. 101–120.

Foucault, M., 1988. Tecnologías del yo. In: Morey, M., ed. *Tecnologías del Yo y Otros Textos Afines*. Barcelona: Ediciones Paidós, pp. 45–94.

Foucault, M., 1990. *The Will to Knowledge: The History of Sexuality Volume 1*. Translated from French by Robert Hurley. London: Penguin.

Foucault, M., 1991. Questions of method. In: Burchell, G., Gordon, C., and Miller, P., eds. *The Foucault Effect: Studies in Governmentality*. Chicago: University of Chicago Press, pp. 73–86.

Foucault, M., 1992. *The Use of Pleasure: The History of Sexuality Volume 2*. Translated from French by Robert Hurley. London: Penguin.

Foucault, M., 1994a. The ethics of the concern for self as a practice of freedom. In: Rabinow, P., ed. *Michel Foucault: Ethics, Subjectivity and Truth*. London: Penguin, pp. 281–302.

Foucault, M., 1994b. Technologies of the self. In: Rabinow, P., ed. *Michel Foucault: Ethics, Subjectivity and Truth*. London: Penguin, pp. 223–251.

Foucault, M., 2009. *Security, Territory, Population*. London: Palgrave MacMillan.

Fuqua, J., Stokols, D., Gress, J., Philips, K., and Harvey, R. 2004. Transdisciplinary collaboration as a basis for enhancing the science and prevention of substance use and 'abuse'. *Substance Use and Misuse*, 39(10–12), pp. 1457–1514.

Gardner, H., 2011. *Creating Minds: An Anatomy of Creativity Seen Through the Lives of Freud, Einstein, Picasso, Stravinsky, Eliot Graham and Gandhi*. 2nd edition. New York: Basic Books.

Gardner, H., Csikszentmihalyi, M., and Damon, W., 2001. *Good Work: When Excellence and Ethics Meet*. New York: Basic Books.

Gilbert, E., 2015. *Big Magic: Creative Living Beyond Fear*. London: Bloomsbury.

Glavenau, V., 2010. Paradigms in the study of creativity: Introducing the perspective of cultural psychology. *New Ideas in Psychology*, 28(1), pp. 79–93.

Goldacre, B., 2003. *Bad Science*. London: Harper Perennial.

Goldie, A., 2015. *The Improv Book: Improvisation for Theatre, Comedy, Education and Life*. London: Oberon Books.

Gordon, C., 1980. *Afterword*. In M. Foucault & C. Gordon (Eds.), Power/Knowledge: Selected Interviews. Brighton, UK: Harvester Press, pp. 229–259.

Gordon, C., 1991. *Governmental Rationality: An Introduction*. In G. Burchell, C. Gordon & P. Miller (Eds.), The Foucault Effect: Studies in Governmentality (pp. 1–51). Chicago, IL: Chicago University Press.

Gruber, H. and Wallace, D., 1999. The case study method and evolving systems approach for understanding unique creative people at work. In: Sternberg, R., ed. *Handbook of Creativity*. Cambridge: Cambridge University Press, pp. 93–115.

Gruber, H. and Wallace, D., 2001. Creative work: The case of Charles Darwin. *American Psychologist*, 56(4), pp. 346–349.

Guildford, J.P., 1950. Creativity. *American Psychologist*, 5(9), pp. 444–454.

Hanson, M.H., 2013. Author, self, monster: Using Foucault to examine functions of creativity. *Journal of Theoretical and Philosophical Psychology*, 33(1), pp. 18–31.

Henman, P., 2010. *Governing Electronically: E-Government and the Reconfiguration of Public Administration, Policy and Power*. Basingstoke (UK): Palgrave McMillan.

Horan, R., 2011. Serendipity. In: Runco, M. and Pritzker, S., eds. *Encyclopaedia of Creativity*. London: Academic Press, pp. 337–344.

Improving Lives, 2017. *Improving Lives: The Future of Work, Health and Disability*. [online] Available at: www.gov.uk/government/publications/improving-lives-the-future-of-work-health-and-disability [Accessed April 2018.]

Jackson, M., 2003. *Creative Holism: Systems Thinking for Managers*. Chichester: John Wiley and Sons.

Kabat-Zinn, J., 2013. *Full Catastrophe Living: Using the Wisdom of Your Body and Mind to Face Stress, Pain and Illness*. New York: Bantam Books Trade Paperbacks.

Kabat-Zinn, J., 2013. *Full Catastrophe Living: Using the Wisdom of Your Body and Mind to Face Stress, Pain, and Illness*. 2nd edition. New York: Bantham Books.

Kaufman, J. and Beghetto, R., 2009. Beyond big and little: The four C model of creativity. *Review of General Psychology*, 13(1), pp. 1–12.

Kaufmann, S., 1995. *At Home with the Universe*. London: Viking.

Kendall, G. & Wickham, G., 1999. *Using Foucault's Methods*. London, UK: Sage.

Khisty, C.J., 2010. The practice of mindfulness for managers in the marketplace. *Systemic Practice and Action Research* 23, pp. 115–125.

Kozbelt, A., Beghetto, R., and Runco, M., 2010. Theories of creativity. In: Sternberg, R., ed. *Handbook of Creativity*. Cambridge: Cambridge University Press, pp. 20–47.

Langer, E., 2014. *Mindfulness*. 25th Anniversary edition. Boston: Da Capo Press.

Lehrer, J., 2012. *Imagine: How Creativity Works*. New York: Houghton Mifflin Harcourt.

Lubart, T., 2001. Models of the creative process: past, present and future. *Creativity research journal*, 13(3–4), pp. 295–308.

Manson, M., 2016. *The Subtle Art of Not Giving a F*ck: A Counterintuitive Approach to Living a Good Life*. New York: HarperCollins Publishers Inc, Harper.

Maturana, H. and Varela, F., 1992. *The Tree of Knowledge: The Biological Roots of Human Understanding*. Boston (US): Shambhala.

Midgley, G., 2000. *Systemic Intervention: Philosophy, Methodology and Practice*. New York: Kluwer Academic/Plenum Publishers.

Moldoveanu, M.C. and Langer, E., 2011. Mindfulness. In: Runco, M. and Pritzker, S., eds. *Encyclopaedia of Creativity*. London: Academic Press, pp. 126–135.

Montuori, A., 2011. Systems approach. In: Runco, M. and Pritzker, S., eds. *Encyclopedia of Creativity*. London: Academic Press, pp. 414–321.

Montuori, A., 2012. Creative inquiry: Confronting the challenges of scholarship in the 21st century. *Futures*, 44, pp. 64–70.

Montuori, A., 2017. The evolution of creativity and the creativity of evolution. *Spanda Journal*, VII(1), pp. 147–156.

Montuori, A. and Purser, R., 1995. Deconstructing the lone genius myth: Toward a contextual view of creativity. *Journal of Humanistic Psychology*, 35(3), pp. 69–112.

Noguera, C., 2009. La gubernamentalidad en los cursos del profesor Foucault. *Revista Educacao & Realidades*, 34, pp. 21–33.

Novotny, H., Scott, P., and Gibbons, M., 2003. Mode 2' revisited: The new production of knowledge – introduction. *Minerva*, 41(3), pp. 179–194.

Oakley, B., 2014. *A Mind for Numbers*. US: Tarcher/Putnam.

Pope, R., 2005. *Creativity: Theory, History and Practice*. London: Routledge.

Puett, M. and Gross-Loh, C., 2016. *The Path: A New Way to Think About Everything*. London: Penguin.

Rhodes, M., 1961. An analysis of creativity. *The Phi Delta Kappan*, 42(7), pp. 305–310.

Richards, R., 2006. Frank Barron and the study of creativity: A voice that lives on. *Journal of Humanistic Psychology*, 46(3), pp. 352–370.

Robinson, K., 2001. *Out of Our Minds: Learning to Be Creative*. Chichester: Capstone Publishing.

Robinson, K. and Aronica, L., 2015. *Creative Schools*. New York: Penguin.

Rose, E., 2013. *On Reflection: An Essay on Technology, Education, and the Status of Thought in the Twenty-First Century*. Toronto: Canadian Scholars' Press Inc.

Rose, N., O'Malley, P., and Valverde, M., 2006. Governmentality. *Annual Review of Law and Social Science* 2, pp. 83–104.

Routledge, R., Gute, G., Gute, D., Nakamura, J., and Csikszentmihalyi, M., 2008. The early lives of highly creative persons: The influence of the complex family. *Creativity Research Journal*, 20(4), pp. 343–357.

Runco, M. and Albert, R., 2010. Creativity research: A historical review. In: Sternberg, R., ed. *Handbook of Creativity*. Cambridge: Cambridge University Press, pp. 3–19.

Runco, M. and Jaeger, G., 2012. The Standard Definition of Creativity. *Creativity Research Journal*, 24(1), pp. 92–96.

Sawyer, K., 2006. *Explaining Creativity: The Science of Human Innovation*. Oxford: Oxford University Press.

Sawyer, K., 2010. Individual and group creativity. In: Sternberg, R., ed. *Handbook of Creativity*. Cambridge: Cambridge University Press, pp. 366–380.

Shaheen, R., 2010. *Creativity in education*. Creative Education, 1(3) pp. 166–169.

Silvia, P. and Kaufman, J., 2010. Creativity and mental illness. In: Sternberg, R., ed. *Handbook of Creativity*. Cambridge: Cambridge University Press, pp. 381–394.

Simonton, D.K., 2011. Eminence. In: Runco, M., and Pritzker, S., ed. 2011. *Encyclopaedia of Creativity*. London: Academic Press, pp. 441–448.

Simonton, D.K., 2012. The science of genius. *Scientific American Mind*, November, pp. 4–11.

Stacey, R., 1996. *Complexity and Creativity in Organisations*. San Francisco: Berrett-Koehler Publishers Inc.

Stahl, J.M. and Brower, R., 2011. Evolving Systems Approach. In: Runco, M., and Pritzker, S., ed. 2011. *Encyclopaedia of Creativity*. London: Academic Press, pp. 476–479.

Stein, M., 1953. Creativity and culture. *The Journal of Psychology*, 36, pp. 311–322.

Sternberg, R., 1999. The concept of creativity: Prospects and paradigms. In: Sternberg, R., ed. 2010. *Handbook of Creativity*. Cambridge: Cambridge University Press, pp. 3–15.

Sternberg, R. and Kaufman, J., 2010. Constraints on creativity: Obvious and not so obvious. In: Sternberg, R., ed. *Handbook of Creativity*. Cambridge: Cambridge University Press, pp. 467–482.

Sternberg, R., 2013. *Reform education: teach wisdom and ethics*. The Phi Delta Kappan 94(7), pp. 44–47.

Sternberg, R. and Lubbart, T., 1992. Buy low and sell high: An investment approach to creativity. *Current Directions in Psychological Science*, 1(1), pp. 1–5.

Stierand, M., Dorfler, V., and MacBryde, J., 2014. Creativity and innovation in Haute Cuisine: Towards a systemic model. *Creativity and Innovation in Haute Cuisine*, 23(1), pp. 15–27.

Takeuchi, H., Taki, Y., Hashizume, H., Sassa, Y., Nagase, T., Nouchi, R., and Kawashima, R., 2012. The association between resting functional connectivity and creativity. *Cerebral Cortex*, 22(12), pp. 2921–2929.

Tang, Y.Y., Holzel, B., and Posner, M., 2015. The neuroscience of mindfulness meditation. *Nature Reviews Neuroscience*, 16(4), pp. 1–13.

Thaler, R., 2009. *Nudge: Improving Decisions About Wealth, Health and Happiness*. London: Penguin.

Torrance, P., 1981. Empirical validation of criterion referenced indicators of creative ability through a longitudinal study. *Creative Child and Adult Quarterly*, 6, pp. 136–140.

Ulrich, W., 1983. *Critical Heuristics of Social Planning: A new Approach to Practical Philosophy*. Bern (Switzerland): Haupt, 1st Edition.

Van Maanen, J., 1988. *Tales of the Field: On Writing Ethnography*. Chicago: The University of Chicago Press.

Varela, F., 1999. *Ethical Know-How: Action, Wisdom and Cognition*. Stanford: Stanford University Press.

Varela, F., Thompson, E., and Rosch, E., 1993. *The Embodied Mind: Cognitive Science and Human Experience*. Cambridge: Massachusetts Institute of Technology Press.

Wallas, G., 1926. *The Art of Thought*. New York: Harcourt, Brace and Company.

Watts, A., 1951. *The Wisdom of Insecurity: A Message for an Age of Anxiety*. New York: Pantheon Books.

Williams, M., Teasdale, J., Segal, Z. and Kabat-Zinn, J., 2007. *The Mindful Way through Depression: Freeing Yourself from Chronic Unhappiness*. London: The Guildford Press.

Wright, R., 2017. *Why Buddhism Is True – The Science and Philosophy of Meditation and Enlightenment*. New York: Simon and Schuster.

Index

Note: page numbers in *italic* indicate a figure and page numbers in **bold** indicate a table on the corresponding page.

For Product Safety Concerns and Information please contact our EU representative GPSR@taylorandfrancis.com Taylor & Francis Verlag GmbH, Kaufingerstraße 24, 80331 München, Germany

Printed and bound by CPI Group (UK) Ltd, Croydon, CR0 4YY

01/05/2025

01858414-0010